COPING WITH DEATH
IN THE FAMILY

TO RACHEL, JED AND LIZA

COPING
WITH
DEATH
IN
THE
FAMILY

GERALD SCHNEIDERMAN M.D.

NC Press Limited
Toronto 1994

Front Cover Design: Jerry Ginsberg
Back Cover Photo: Albert Gilbert

Fourth Edition 1994
© Gerald Schneiderman, 1994

Canadian Cataloguing in Publication Data

Schneiderman, Gerald.
  Coping with death in the family

Includes bibliographical references and index.
ISBN 1-055021-076-9

1. Death – Psychological aspects. 2. Bereavement -
Psychological aspects.   I. Title. II. Series.

BF789.04536   1994   155.9'37   C94-930932-X

We would like to thank the Ontario Arts Council, the Ontario Publishing Centre, the Ontario Ministry of Culture, Tourism and Recreation, Toronto Hospital for Sick Children, the Canada Council and the Government of Canada, Department of Communications, for their assistance in the production of this book.

New Canada Publications, a division of NC Press Limited, Box 452, Station A, Toronto, Ontario, Canada, M5W 1H8.

Printed and bound in Canada

CONTENTS

*All profits from the sale of this book,
including author's royalties, are being donated
to The Toronto Hospital for Sick Children.*

ACKNOWLEDGMENT

The writing of this book evolved from my research on genetic disease in conjunction with the Departments of Biochemistry and Psychiatry at the Hospital for Sick Children. I would like to thank Dr. J. Alexander Lowden and Dr. Quentin Rae-Grant for assisting in the research which led to the writing of this book.

In addition, I am grateful for the support of many professional colleagues and friends during my writing. In particular, I would like to thank Dr. Graham Berman, the late Dr. John Cleghorn, Dr. Nathan Epstein and Mr. Justice Allan Goodman.

I am indebted to Dr. William Feldman, Dr. Susan Tallett and Patricia Winders, R.N. of the Department of General Pediatrics at the Hospital for Sick Children for their encouragement and enthusiasm in our research group.

I appreciate the interest of Caroline Walker of NC Press, who supported the fourth edition of the book and suggested the addition of a new chapter.

Gerald Schneiderman, M.D.
Toronto, Ontario
February 1994

INTRODUCTION

The only certainty in life is death. It is universal – we are all affected by it during our lives, and we will all be its victim one day. Our reactions to death are as individual as our own lives but are at the same time, similar in many ways. This book is intended to help the bereaved understand some of their intense reactions, reassure them that other people have felt this way, and give practical advice on how to cope with the death and carry on with their own lives. There is also one chapter on dealing with your own death since watching our friends and family die, reminds us of our own mortality.

In my clinical practice I see the intense pain and suffering that death causes every day for the survivors. Adults may develop emotional problems or turn to drugs and alcohol in an attempt to ease the pain, and children may develop physical or behavioral problems because they cannot accept the death of a parent, brother or sister. These people are not suffering a mental disorder. Their ability to function has not been impaired because they have not recovered from the shock of death. This book is intended to help them and in some cases tell them where they can seek more help.

After the death of someone close, some people consult a psychiatrist because they may be suffering depression and may feel that life is no longer worth living. Working with the patients for weeks, months or years, psychiatrists help them overcome the paralyzing effect that death has had on their lives. However, most people deal with their grief alone and do not get professional help if they are having problems. It is hoped this book will show them that they are not alone and that all over the world people are experiencing the same fears and anxieties.

Even though we all come from varying ethnic backgrounds, practice different religions, and live in different communities, there is a certain universality to grief and mourning. This book does not deal with the various rituals practiced by different groups when death occurs nor the variations in mourning or funerals. It does deal with the emotions that all people, regardless of origin, experience when they lose someone close. We are basically all the same, and losing a father or a wife in North America will produce the same void in the survivors as it does in Africa.

This is a common sense guide for all age groups on how to live with the loss of a loved one. It does not provide magical cures for depression, nor can it eradicate loneliness, but it is hoped it can give the strength and reassurance necessary to cope with the difficulties of bereavement. An important message is that regardless of the pain and hurt, survivors have a responsibility to carry on and pursue life to its fullest. The living can also draw inspiration from the dead and strength from the experience of coping with death. The book also includes constructive suggestions for friends and family about how they can best help the survivors.

This book is intended primarily for the family. The stronger the unit, the better equipped it is to deal with problems, and the easier it will be for the surviving members to complete their mourning.

If the climate of the family has always been one in which the mother and father have been honest with each other and have worked at their marriage, chances are they have transmitted their openness and commitment to their children. If the children can come to their parents when difficulties arise and get assistance, they will feel secure enough to go to them in times of crisis. This becomes very important when a death occurs. In families where there is division and abuse among the members, a death may mark the end of the unit. If the parents and children are not prepared to support and help one another through a crisis, the family may just as well break apart, and in many cases it does.

Families who are committed to staying together must be realistic after a death and realize there are difficult times ahead. If it was a parent who died, the family must restructure and reallocate roles. A death in the family should not mean the end of the family. This book tries to offer hope to families and show that although death is tragic, life can and must go on for the survivors.

I

DEATH OF AN INFANT

A century ago, it was not unusual for a mother to experience the death of one or more of her children. Infant mortality rates were high, about one in six newborns died. Today, however, people are shocked to hear of infant deaths, and the mortality rate among newborns is about one in one hundred. Most people never experience nor expect to experience the death of an infant and as a result, such deaths seem doubly shocking. Despite the technological advances of modern medicine however, some babies still die, frequently as premature infants, although also from congenital malformations, asphyxiation, birth injuries, influenza, pneumonia and other infections.

During the first few months of life an infant is totally helpless in providing for itself and can communicate with its caregivers only by crying. Because it is too early for a baby's eventual strengths and weaknesses to show themselves, parents tend to pin their hopes and aspirations, realistic and otherwise, on their baby. Parents can hope that a baby will excel academically or in athletics, music, or art; in fact, they can let their imaginations run wild simply because there is nothing at this stage to prove them wrong. The realities of course come later when the politician becomes a printer, the concert pianist turns tuner and the hockey star cannot skate. As children grow older and begin to communicate their own feelings about what they are and what they want to be, parental fantasies give way to harsh realities. Parents who lose a child of four or five know exactly what they are losing. On the other hand, when a baby dies the family's hopes and dreams have not been tested and the death always leaves the sadness of what might have been.

People have babies for a variety of reasons. These can be assessed, in turn, to determine exactly what the death of a baby actually means. Many people, when asked, indicate that their desire to have babies is linked to a desire to perpetuate the family name and tradition. In this attempt to continue the generations, many people feel they will achieve a kind of immortality themselves and will live on through their children and grandchildren.

For some people, having children represents an attempt to resolve their own memories of an unhappy childhood. As a result, they derive a great deal of satisfaction from having and loving children and from being loved in return, and often, in a sense, use their children to repair the damage of the past. Other couples feel incomplete without children, are anxious to share their own love and joy with a child and are able to accept the frustration and anger which children can generate as well.

Finally, some people look upon children as a kind of second chance and hope that they will succeed where the parents have failed. A parent who was not accepted into medical school may fully intend to encourage and, in fact, push his offspring to be a doctor. Parents expect their babies to become attractive in appearance and to carry on and often to improve upon their values and lifestyle. When a baby dies, there is not a parent anywhere whose hopes and expectations are not shattered by the experience.

The unexpected death of an infant is an exceedingly painful experience for a family to endure. One mother, just after the death of her three-week-old daughter, described it in this way:

> For nine months my baby had been growing inside me. I could feel her kicking and could hardly wait for the day she was born to hold her and love her. It was the saddest day of my life when she died. She was born with a congenital malformation – something was wrong with her digestive system. She died before I even brought her home from the hospital. For a few months afterwards, I used to cry when-

ever I was with a mother who was holding a baby. I had an overwhelming urge to grab the baby from its mother's arms and hold it close. My arms ached for a child.

This woman already had a five-year-old son but wanted to have a large family. Unfortunately, she was never able to conceive another child and the memory of her tragic loss has haunted her throughout the years.

Some men, when their babies die, lose all self-esteem and begin to blame themselves for being unable to produce a baby which would survive. One young man dropped out of law school after his baby son died. He lost all his self-confidence and his feelings of impotence carried into his career. Dropping out of law school also served another function – it was his way of punishing himself for what had happened. He felt guilty about his baby's death and this was his way of paying for it. Unfortunately, like many other parents in his situation, this man was distorting reality. Dropping his career could in no way pay for his son's death or bring him back.

Some women, after the death of an infant, want to become pregnant again right away, perhaps in an attempt to prove themselves capable of producing a child who will live.

Similarly, fathers whose infants die often view it as an affront to their masculinity and sometimes indulge in affairs with other women. This is often an attempt to prove that they can produce a perfect child with another woman. This, of course, puts the blame for the death on the wife and puts additional strain on the marital relationship.

Usually though, the burden of the guilt falls on the mother who has carried the infant through pregnancy and is usually the primary caregiver. If a baby is born deformed, the mother will inevitably begin to assume a role of responsibility. In the case of a premature birth, a mother may question her ability to maintain a pregnancy. A mother, who has had a previous abortion may convince herself that she is being punished. In addition, sudden infant deaths often bring questions from the police and from hospital personnel and frequent criticism from other family members.

Every family facing the death of a baby must deal not only with its grief for the dead child but must face new problems and conflicts in the family setting as well. The ability to deal with the death is often a function of the prior emotional strength of the family. In poorly adjusted families, where relationships are already precarious, the death of an infant often marks the death of the family unit. Such was the case of Mr. and Mrs. C. They had separated twice, but both times got back together because they had nothing else. Thinking that a baby would help their troubled marriage, Mrs. C. became pregnant. The baby was born and two months later died in an unexplained crib death. After the death Mrs. C. became very depressed and had uncontrollable crying spells. Her husband, who had never been a talker, withdrew completely and would not even acknowledge her presence at times. Occasionally, when he did speak to her, it was in angry outburst, blaming her for the baby's death. Their own parents did not console them, but instead made matters worse by blaming them both for what had happened. Eventually this couple could no longer endure life together and got a divorce.

Although many of the deaths which strike infants occur with little or no warning, there are other diseases, genetic in origin, in which there is a time lag between the actual diagnosis and the death. While it is devastating for a family to have to come to grips with the death of an infant, it is probably far more difficult to cope with the knowledge that, at some point in the near future, an infant will die, and there is nothing that medical science can do to prevent it.

In the early 1900s, approximately five deaths per one thousand live births occurred in Canada and the United States as a result of genetic diseases. Even today, despite immense progress in the field of medicine, this figure remains virtually unchanged. Although a great deal of progress has been made in the detection of such diseases, very little headway has been made in terms of curing them.

Every cell in the human body contains, in its nucleus,

forty-six chromosomes, each of which contains a code which
determines traits in the offspring such as skin, hair and eye
colour and stature. During human reproduction, a process of
cell division called *meiosis* takes place. This process of meiosis
leaves a sperm and an ovum containing twenty-three chromosomes each, half the number in other body cells. During conception, a fertilized ovum containing forty-six chromosomes is
formed, and the sex of the offspring is determined by either an
X chromosome (Female) or a Y chromosome (Male) from the
sperm. Similarly, each of the remaining chromosomes seeks
out its appropriate partner so that all chromosomes are in
pairs, as they are in all body cells. With the genes (or codes) of
each chromosome which act in either a dominant or a reces-
sive manner, a particular offspring is, quite literally, con-
structed. Thus, a dark-haired man married to a blond woman
may produce a dark-haired child if the dark-haired genes are
dominant or a blond child if the appropriate genes are dominant.

In a similar manner, people can be carriers of defective
genes which do not affect them personally but which may affect their offspring. If both parents are carriers of a defective
gene, there is one chance in four that their baby will actually
have the genetic disease or be completely free of it and two
chances in four that the baby will be a carrier. Until recently,
it was impossible to know whether or not a child would be
affected by a genetic disorder. In the case of Mr. and Mrs. O.,
two of their children died before the parents became aware of
the fact that they were, indeed, carriers.

Mr. and Mrs. O.'s first child was born two months premature, and everyone attributed her continual poor health to
that. As Mrs. O. said:

> She cried night and day, and was never a normal healthy
> baby. We had an awful feeling right from birth that some-
> thing was very wrong with her, but everyone kept reassur-
> ing us that she would outgrow her problems.
>
> When we finally brought her home from the hospital, we

had a very hard time with her. We wanted her to get better so desperately, but she continued to cry all the time. She was in and out of hospital, and at six months, she took a turn for the worse. The doctors did not know exactly what was wrong with her, but they knew she was dying of some sort of brain disease.

It's very eerie when all of a sudden you find out your child is going to die. Your first born. At first you don't believe it. My mother called me that evening we heard the diagnosis. I can remember the only thing going through my mind is she's going to die, but how do you tell somebody your daughter is going to die? It can't happen. How does a little baby die? It's not right. We were just torn apart. I remember crying and walking around in a complete fog. We couldn't believe it was happening to us. It was almost like a terrible movie. How can those things happen in real life? After all, we are normal healthy people. We cried each time we went to the hospital and saw our little baby girl deteriorating a bit more. We felt so helpless. She was dying in front of our eyes, and there was nothing we could do for her. She remained in hospital for seven months, and finally died when she was thirteen months old.

At the time of their daughter's death Mrs. O. was three months pregnant. She did not know that the death had been caused by a rare genetic disease, and was very happy that very soon a new baby would be born. Whenever she felt sad about losing her daughter, she was comforted by the thought that the new baby would help her get over her loss.

Their next child was born a seemingly healthy baby. His parents showered him with love and care and thought he was the greatest baby ever born.

Unlike our daughter, John never cried, and gave us tremendous pleasure those first few months. I got closer to him than I did to our daughter because I breast fed him, and he responded to me so much more. As he started to develop, we watched him carefully for any signs of illness. At the time, we still did not know why our daughter died, and our doctor reassured us that John was fine. When he was about six months old, his head started to droop. This was one of the first symptoms we had seen in his sister a year earlier, and suddenly we feared the worst. The doctor saw him immediately, and those few minutes when he examined him seemed like to hours to us. When he came out, he shook his head sadly and confirmed our worst fears.

All we could think of was why us again, wasn't one enough. We got into the car and my husband started pounding the dashboard. He just pounded and pounded until he had used up all his strength. Then he broke down and wept. He started screaming, "I thought God was supposed to love little children. How could he do this to us again. Oh God, are you really there?" We had lost all faith, and knew there really was no justice in the world. All we wanted was a normal baby, and for us that seemed to be impossible. People all around the world are blessed with healthy children, then some people turn around and batter their own children, or even kill them. Some women get pregnant, and then have abortions because they don't want a child. It made us so angry to think about all the people who didn't want children or who mistreated them, when we wanted one so badly.

Many people when faced with the loss of an infant start to question the existence of God. They can't rationalize how a benevolent God could allow such a thing to happen to someone so young and innocent. Eventually that anger dissipates as people start to cope with the death, but some people can never again believe in the existence of God.

Eventually Mr. and Mrs. O.'s anger and bitterness mellowed into acceptance of the realities. They knew that John only had a few more months to live, and wanted him with them until the end. They decided not to hospitalize him, and tried to make him as comfortable and happy as possible in his own home. Mr. O. took time off work to be with his dying son, and helped his wife with her sorrow. They both felt responsible for what had happened, although they did not blame one another. Keeping John at home and caring for him there was their way of relieving their own sadness. John's presence, painful as it was, helped them come to an acceptance of the eventual outcome. In addition to their son's serious medical problems, they were faced with the psychological problems of facing their own child's death for a second time.

> As he got sicker, and lost more muscle control, we had to start tube feedings, because he could no longer eat the normal way. I had been a nurse, so I knew the procedure. My husband wanted to help too, so I taught him how to insert the tubes and clean them. Each feeding took two hours, and there were two feedings a day. John was very brave throughout, and even managed to smile now and then. We could see in his eyes that he knew we were there with him and helping him.

> During those seven months, we rarely went out because we were so occupied with our son. We couldn't leave him with anyone, because people were afraid he would die when we were away. Because we couldn't go out, our friends had to come to visit us at home. Some never came, and never even acknowledged the fact that there was a dying child at home. Others did come, but said things like, "Let's not talk about John." The friends we treasured were those who came over, and weren't afraid to see him or talk about him. At the time, he was our whole life, and not to talk about him was unnatural. We didn't need to be cheered up. We were fine. All we wanted for our friends was to stand by us, and come and see us once in a while. We were so cut off, and they were the only link we had with the rest of the world.

Adapting to the loss of an infant is a very difficult task. If your family life is emotionally healthy, then you and your spouse will be able to resolve problems when they occur. When troubles arise, you won't have to count on friends and relatives as much as on each other for help. This is precisely what happened in this household. Mrs. O. got her greatest help from her husband.

During those months, my husband's love kept me going. Even though we were going through a trying time, we were still able to get pleasure from sex. I unintentionally got pregnant again, and decided I could not put another child and ourselves through this misery once again. Although all my life I have been against abortion, I now felt this was the only way out. Just before I had the abortion, I lost all faith and all hope, and I wanted to kill myself. I was crossing a bridge with my husband, and I lost control. For a moment I went crazy, and tried to throw myself off the bridge. If my husband had not been there, I might have succeeded. He saved me. He loves me dearly, and I love him. He saved my life and my sanity. Without him I couldn't have gone on living.

Before John died, my husband took seven weeks off work to be at home with us. We spent every moment together, it was as if every moment we had with our son was too precious to waste. We knew the end was near as John became weaker and weaker and couldn't even tolerate the tube feedings. When he died, my husband was holding him in his arms, and I was by his side. It was not as we had imagined it would be. It was not frightening or gruesome, it was very gentle and peaceful. John just closed his eyes, and it was over. We held him and rocked him for awhile, and then kissed him goodbye through our tears.

By that time Mr. and Mrs. O. knew the reason for their children's deaths. When John got sick the hospital did extensive testing on him to try to discover what was wrong. They found that he was suffering from an extremely rare genetic disease, which had killed their daughter too. Neither Mr. O. nor Mrs. O. knew that they were carriers of this defective gene. If they had known, they could have been spared a lot of anguish and would have adopted children right away. Their chances were one in four of having a child who would die, and both times it happened. As Mrs. O. put it:

It seemed that fate was against us, and we decided that we should adopt a child. About a year later, we adopted a little boy, and it made such a difference to our lives. It brought life and joy back into our home. We never believed people who said they loved their adopted child as much as their own, but now we do. We just worship him, and undoubtedly we spoil him rotten. He's such a relaxed and bright little fellow and quite remarkably he bears a strong resemblance to our little John.

Two years after the adoption they learned of a new procedure called amniocentesis, which can determine certain abnormalities in the fetus. Their doctor convinced them to try to have a child of their own, because this new procedure could be reliably used on the mother at an early stage in the pregnancy:

> We took a chance and we now have a lovely baby daughter. We still cry sometimes when we think about our two dead children, but it's hard to remain sad when you have two happy, healthy children romping around the house.

Mr. and Mrs. O. have unquestionably suffered more than a fair share of pain and grief but have emerged with a deeper and stronger bond of love between them and a greater appreciation of each other and their children.

In coping with their own grief over the death of their infant, parents should be encouraged to spend some time in mourning and accepting the death and in coming to grips with their anger before attempting another pregnancy. Probably six to twelve months is a reasonable length of time and will likely diminish the desire to replace the dead baby. It is essential that a subsequent pregnancy be undertaken out of a genuine desire for another baby and not a replacement. If the infant's death has been the result of a genetic disease, it is essential the doctor be closely involved before pregnancy is begun. Amniocentesis, a procedure whereby fluid surrounding the fetus can be examined for abnormalities, can be used. This can allow time for a therapeutic abortion should the fetus appear to be abnormal.

It is important for parents who are caring for a dying child or who are actually grieving for a dead child to cope with the sadness of the other children in the family as well. Parents of a dying infant who can no longer be helped by medical or surgical procedures may want to consider caring for the baby at home. It can prove upsetting for other children who will inevitably receive less attention than the patient, but should be considered.

It is helpful for parents providing home care for a dying infant to arrange for an occasional babysitter. Potential babysitters are often reluctant to help out of fear that the baby might die while they are caring for it. Thus, parents must encourage such help to feel comfortable in the home and make every attempt to reassure them that they will not be blamed if that should, in fact, happen.

Parents often reflect their own anxieties about death by attempting to protect their children from knowing about it. Children often do encounter death at an early age however, and have every right to expect that their parents will be honest in talking about it.

Children should certainly be given factual information about death and in particular, why their brother or sister died and whether he or she was buried or cremated. Of course, explanations about death and beliefs about an afterlife and the soul will vary with culture and attitudes. But there should be no attempt to fabricate stories as children's understanding is often very literal. To say the "baby has gone on a long trip" or is "up in the sky" simply invites a youngster to await the traveller's return. It is equally dangerous to equate sickness with death. It is very easy to say, "The baby was very sick and she died," but children then tend to confuse a simple cold or viral infection with their own impending death.

The funeral itself is an excellent opportunity for children to take part in the mourning process. Although funerals for children are often private family ceremonies, it is a matter of personal preference. Certainly, children who have reached the age of seven or eight should be allowed, and should in fact be encouraged, to attend. Even younger children should not be kept away if they are insistent. It is a ritual in which children can observe their parents' sadness and express some of their own grief. No child, however, should be forced to attend a funeral if he or she would prefer not to do so.

Perhaps the most important advice for parents who have lost a baby is to encourage them to comfort and not blame each other. Grieving over the death takes a great deal of time and it is often disrupted by attempts to attach blame for the death and thus rationalize the loss somewhat. Some events however, have no basis in logic or rationality – they just happen. The grieving process, no matter how painful, should not be interrupted by bitterness; nor should the growth of the family be paralyzed by fear. With time, energy, and the mutual respect of family members, the pain and injury which result from a baby's death can be endured and the wounds repaired.

II
THE DYING CHILD

The death of a child must surely be one of the most devastating experiences to be endured by a family. While all of the feelings it engenders in the survivors, the sadness, the guilt, and the anger, are not unique, they can be infinitely more destructive than a death which occurs at any other stage in the life of a family. Children are simply not supposed to die. On a rational level one can accept the death of the elderly in terms of their age, the fullness of their life, or as relief from a lengthy illness. Similarly the death of an infant can often be reasoned in terms of a premature birth or a genetic defect. It is no less painful, but is perhaps more readily accepted.

In the highly developed nations of the world, however, children are expected to be healthy and energetic, to have chicken pox, and recover – they are expected to grow up. Thus, when a child dies, the event is so shocking and so repulsive to our established pattern of life and death, that the damage to the survivors can often be irreparable.

More children between the ages of one and fourteen years die from accidents than from any other cause. In fact, over half of the deaths in this age group can be attributed to accidental causes. It goes without saying that when a child dies accidentally the burden on the surviving family members cannot be measured in terms of the loss alone. The guilt, either real or imagined, which inevitably accompanies the accidental death of a child, can be far more destructive in the long term than the actual death. The child killed by a car while bicycling around the block, the child who drowns in the neighbour's swimming pool, the child propelled through the windshield of a car in a traffic accident – these are all senseless deaths which can torture those involved indefinitely. It is exceedingly difficult because not only must each of the survivors bear and resolve his individual feelings of guilt, but each must, in addition, be prepared to deal with the accompanying hostility which is very often an attempt to "lay the blame," rationalize the death, and thus lessen the agony. This is small consolation, however, for the survivor (very often the mother) who is the focus of the hostility and simultaneously torn by guilt. While it may be inevitable that such a family prolong the grieving process by indulging in the fantasy of "If only . . . ," there is a point at which fantasizing becomes a useless and, in fact, a self-destructive exercise. Life is, at best, a risky proposition, and the guilt and anger must eventually fade in the face of the knowledge that beyond a certain point, families simply cannot control the lives of their members and parents cannot protect their children from all harm.

On the other hand, the loss of a child through an illness such as cancer (which is the second major killer of children) has an entirely different impact. Although one has time to become accustomed to the knowledge that a child is dying, it is much more difficult to accept terminal illness in a child.

When a child dies accidentally it is nearly always possible to establish a cause and effect relationship, a speeding car, an unlocked gate, or an unfastened seat belt. For the family, and particularly for the parents of a child stricken with a terminal illness, there is no rational explanation. There is total bewilderment when parents ask, "Why my child? Why not some other child?" Again there is the tremendous guilt which occurs when the parents inevitably begin to question their own degree of responsibility. There is often the initial assumption that a child's illness is punishment, perhaps for inadequate prenatal care, for poor nutrition, or even for leaving a child frequently with a babysitter. On one level the family members know perfectly well that this kind of guilt is unfounded, but on another level they are desperately looking for anything which will tell them why their child is going to die. Finally there is the anger – an anger which is difficult to focus but which is simply an expression of the unfairness and injustice of having to watch one's child suffer and die.

The grieving for the death of a child is particularly exhausting, because it begins long before the child actually dies and often comes at a time when parents have responsibilities to other children. The family's initial reaction to the news that a child is dying is one of absolute disbelief, and often precious energy is dissipated in searching for other doctors, other diagnoses and proof of "wonder cures." Such was the case of Mr. and Mrs. McIntyre, a young couple whose son, Tommy, was diagnosed as having leukemia:

> If someone said to you, your child is going to die in six months, you would tell them they're crazy, because you can't believe this nightmare is happening to you.
>
> For the next few weeks, I tried to pretend that Tommy was actually improving. One day one of the children on the ward said, "Why can't Tommy ride a bike like me?" I responded by saying, "Well, he's in here for some more treatments. We're fighting this thing, and he's going to get better, aren't you, Tommy?"
>
> Although Tommy was only four years old, he seemed to sense what was happening to him. He turned to me and said, "I don't know, Mommy, I just don't know."

It soon became apparent, however, that Tommy was not improving. Once his mother could no longer deny the inevitable course of his illness, she began to bargain for his life, a remarkably common occurrence among families faced with death:

> At the beginning, you do a lot of funny things to try to help your child. I used to have a recurring dream, that if I made two thousand peanut butter sandwiches everything would be alright. I guess a part of me was bargaining with God, for Tommy's life. "If I do this, can I have my child back?" When I woke up from that dream I used to think that God

was trying to tell me that if I did something for him, he would make Tommy well again. I would have tried anything to make my son well again, but, despite all my prayers and good deeds, Tommy was gradually getting worse. In our family Tommy was the only child, the only son, the only grandchild, and the only great-grandchild. If love could have cured him, he would have been very healthy.

When the bargaining failed, Mrs. McIntyre became very depressed because she realized that nothing could help her son. In addition, her sadness was magnified by the knowledge that her son seemed to know what was happening to him:

Tommy knew he was in trouble, because he could pick it up all around him. His doctor would come into the room and talk to us about what had worked and what hadn't. He talked about remission and chemotherapy, and the child picked this all up and then he worried too. Tommy worried about the family as well. One of his grandfathers visited him with a very sad expression. From across the room, Tommy walked over to him, touched his hand and said, "Don't worry about me, Grandpa, don't be sad about me." It was moments like that which made me scream with rage at the injustice of life. Why was our little boy dying when other children, all around us, were happy, healthy, and normal?

Although families may react differently during the course of a terminal illness, a fairly common reaction is to suddenly begin focusing attention and lavishing gifts on the dying child. These excesses often arise from a genuine desire to please the dying child. However, they may also stem from the parents' own feeling of guilt about their relationship with the child, combined with the knowledge that their last chance to show their love and affection is rapidly dwindling. Some children, during periods of remission, may thoroughly enjoy special outings and trips, although not in a manner which singles them out as receiving preferential treatment. Frankly, the majority of such children are happier at home, in familiar surroundings and in a fairly regular routine, with people who can not only love and care for them, but who will listen to and cry with them as well.

Some reactions, however, are so cruel and bizarre that they almost defy description or belief. One couple reacted to the news of their son's illness by dressing themselves and the child entirely in black. Needless to say, the child was terrified, and his last months became a nightmare.

Unfortunately there is a tendency to concentrate solely on the dying child and on the relationships between the child and those who are directly involved in caring for him. Often this serves only to neglect the remaining members of the family who must reshape their lives not only during the illness, but after the actual death as well. The mother is often the person most directly involved with the sick child, either at home or in hospital. Thus the father may begin to feel isolated within the sadness that permeates the family and may sense that he is intruding upon the special relationship which exists between the sick child and those who are actually nursing him. Many fathers, as a result, begin to spend more and more time away from home, often at work. The premise may be that more work will provide more money to ensure that the sick child is well looked after. In reality the father simply cannot tolerate the oppressive sadness that surrounds the sick child and is attempting to escape it.

In addition, the remaining healthy children may suffer during the course of their brother's or sister's illness. They may resent the care and attention given the dying child. They too, may harbour terrible guilt feelings, particularly if they have wished, in a moment of anger, that their brother or sister would become ill and die. Such a child is absolutely horrified and panic-stricken to see his wish come true and thus may assume all the blame for the illness himself. Children may also become frightened about their own health, and assume that they will be the next to die. Brothers and sisters of the dying child may manifest these fears in a variety of ways, depending on their ability to accept the situation and on their ability to express their feelings about it. They may become depressed, do poorly at school or have difficulty sleeping. They may also display a variety of physical symptoms as well, including headaches, stomach aches and wet beds.

Mr. and Mrs. Simon had two daughters, aged eight and five years. The elder daughter, Susan, had been ill with cancer for several years.

Mary had been sent to her grandmother's house off and on during her sister's illness, as her parents found it difficult to cope when Susan felt very sick. Mary had been taken to her grandmother's house during the last two weeks of her sister's life, having no inkling that her sister was about to die. She was not taken to the funeral and was told only that her sister had "gone to sleep forever." Very shortly, of course, Mary began to have difficulty sleeping and to experience terrible nightmares. Sleep, in her mind, became equated with death. She was absolutely convinced that she would be next, and was furious with her parents for not wakening Susan after she had fallen asleep.

This is a perfect example of how a family, unwittingly trying to afford security and protection, can create monumental distortions and anxieties in the mind of a child. One should never lie to a child about death. It is terribly important for parents, despite the awesome burden of caring for a dying child, to understand and hopefully to anticipate these kinds of feelings. It is the open, honest family, in which caring and respect are simply taken for granted, which survives such tragedies and often renews itself in the process.

Depending on their age, children probably face their own impending death in a far more realistic way than do their families. Young children simply do not understand the whole concept of death and are most distressed about leaving favourite toys or pets behind. For most children under the age of four, who are often terrified of being abandoned, the presence of familiar faces is perhaps their greatest comfort. Tension in this age group is often relieved by motor activity (such as jumping, running and wiggling) which should be accepted and encouraged.

The six or seven year old child is often curious about his disease and seeks information which should be answered in a straightforward and realistic way. The point at which a child begins to have difficulty accepting his own death is at the age of about ten years. At this stage of their development children are becoming very aware of the world around them and of their place in it; they are beginning to grasp their own potential and may be beginning to formulate long term plans or goals. It is very important, here, for families to continue to communicate openly with the dying child, so that real feelings and especially fears can be shared and thus partially resolved.

The point at which the terminally ill child actually dies is one of extraordinary emotion. There is an indescribable sadness in knowing that a child's life has ended, but there are many other emotions which are mingled with the sadness as well. There is often an extension of the anger that was experienced during the child's illness, which at this stage is often directed towards the doctors and hospital personnel who have been involved. Such was the case with Tommy's mother:

> Tommy went into hospital for the last time, just after Christmas. Before he went in, he said to me, "I would like to see my Christmas toys just one more time." He seemed to know that he would never come home again.

During Tommy's final stay in hospital, Mrs. McIntyre described the hospital staff moving him from room to room an aspect of his hospital stay which upset him tremendously:

> At first he was in a ward with other children and had lots of playmates. As he worsened, he was moved to a semi-private room. Naturally, Tommy cried because he didn't want to leave the other children, and couldn't understand why he was being shifted from room to room. The doctors seemed insensitive to his feelings and shifted him to a private room just before his death. This, of course, terrified him, as he was afraid of being alone.

Mrs. McIntyre was at the hospital when her son died. She described it in this way:

> When Tommy died, I was holding him in my arms. A nurse quickly ushered me out of the room. I remember my feet moving, but I wasn't screaming. For your child's sake you remain very calm. I kept telling them that I wanted to go back into his room, but they wouldn't let me. It was a terminal ward, and perhaps they were afraid that I would become hysterical. I was not allowed to go back and I couldn't seem to make people understand what I wanted. It was my way of saying goodbye to my little boy. Even if I could have gone back and let loose, it would have been better. I pleaded to be left alone in the room . . . let me cry, let me do anything, but they wouldn't let me. I was put into a small room near the nurses' station and remained shut away there until my husband arrived, and then we were driven home.

Hospitals and hospital staff members are becoming more enlightened in their care of the dying. However in a well-intentioned attempt to protect the survivors (as in the case of Mrs. McIntyre) and to deal with the death in a routine manner, the entire grieving process may be disrupted. Mrs. McIntyre obviously felt she had been deprived of the opportunity to say goodbye to Tommy in a way that would be satisfying to her.

Another very common emotion, which surrounds the death of a child, is that of relief and thus guilt. It is only natural, after months and perhaps years of sickness, after suffering and disrupted family life, to feel relieved that the nightmare has ended:

> Although I could never have said so at the time, it was a relief when Tommy died. His suffering was incredible, but the lack of complaining was unbelievable. At the time I felt guilty for feeling relief, because there is a lot of guilt tied into your child's death. But nobody tells you that you're going to feel it, so don't worry about it. Part of my guilt was because I felt responsible for him – after all, maybe I had done something wrong when I was pregnant, maybe I had eaten something dangerous. I was vainly searching for the answer to the big question – why?

Survivors must realize that these feelings are normal and should be expressed openly and without guilt. When a child dies the family is no longer whole. A part of the structure is missing, so the survivors must reconcile the loss either by reshaping the entire family unit or by reworking their own roles within it. In some cases emotions are so volatile and the emptiness so profound that family members can no longer tolerate life as a unit. This often happens in a situation where a husband and wife find it difficult to communicate with and to comfort each other. After Tommy's death, Mr. and Mrs. McIntyre had to struggle to repair a damaged relationship under the strain of being unable to talk to one another:

> I'm a talker and I think that saved me. I talked to my family. I cried until I was all cried out. It's much harder if you can't express it. Every so often my husband would let himself go with me, and then all the stored-up rage and bitterness would pour out like a flood and he would shake and weep uncontrollably. He's not much of a talker though, and that's a problem.

> Unfortunately, my husband didn't have anyone other than me to help him cope with his sadness. His mother never comforted him when he really needed her. She never went to him and hugged him and said, "I'm really sorry, son." Because he didn't receive any emotional support from his family, and because of his natural tendency to keep his feelings to himself, he has had a much more difficult time in coming to terms with the death.

The McIntyres were fortunate in seeking professional help after their child's illness, so that although the family continued to function under a great deal of strain, the death of Tommy did not signal the death of the family. The multitude of emotions surrounding the death of a child cannot be wished away, nor do they disappear if ignored. They eventually surface and take their toll if not expressed and dealt with in an honest and open way.

Other families are not so fortunate, and in refusing to reconcile themselves to their child's death in order to allow the grieving process to heal their sadness and rage, they surround themselves with fantasies.

One couple, who lost their only child, never mentioned her name again. The parents were the type of people who withdrew if something was bothering them, and their tendency was to avoid problems by simply hoping they would disappear. They found it exceedingly difficult to deal with any unpleasant situation by facing it. When their daughter died in a fire, they suffered terribly, but could not tell each other about these innermost thoughts. Even as time went on, they maintained the charade – it was as if they had never had a child. Of course, both the mother and father were thinking about her constantly, and their hidden feelings eventually surfaced in the form of terrible nightmares.

On the other hand, some families choose the other extreme and continue to live as if a tragedy had never occurred.

Mrs. Blackburn kept her dead daughter's room exactly as she had left it. For years the bed, the clothes and the toys were simply left as they were. Typical comments from Mrs. Blackburn were, "If only poor Jenny had not been taken from me she would have been seventeen years old now. It's hard to believe I could have a seventeen-year-old daughter already." This woman had never been able to say goodbye to her dead child. Her family, in permitting, and in fact, encouraging the fantasy to continue, suffered as much as she did.

Living with sadness is a very personal matter, but talking about the tragedy kept the drama constantly alive and hid any feelings of guilt and anger which this mother probably felt. In a sense, she was protecting herself. Once she had acknowledged the fact that Jenny was really dead, she would have had to face her deepest feeling about life and death. Putting an end to the fantasy would necessarily have forced the death into its proper perspective.

Once the fact of death has been accepted the healing process can begin in earnest. The anger, the guilt and the depression take a very long time to dissipate, and there are often times when families wonder if any semblance of normalcy will ever return to their lives. Many people find that talking or crying can be a great source of comfort, or that physical activity (such as tennis or jogging) sometimes helps.

Often other members of the family and close friends can and should help by talking, or more particularly by listening. A sincere offer to babysit children or to help with housework is often appreciated.

One temptation to which the grieving family often succumbs is the desire to replace the dead child as soon as possible. Parents should not attempt to adopt a child or to begin another pregnancy immediately, as such spontaneous actions can bring feelings of regret, damaging to both parents and children. Families should wait at least several months, and if adoption or pregnancy still seems feasible, it should be pursued as an honest desire for another child, and not as a substitute for the one who has died. Mrs. McIntyre described their family in subsequent years:

> We had another son a year after Tommy died, and we found ourselves making comparisons all the time. It's not really fair because no one can ever replace another person. You have to come to terms with the fact that your child is dead, and you can't try to make him live on through your other children. Three years later we had another son and our two boys mean everything to us. Although we don't dwell on the past we have never forgotten that terrible time when Tommy died. It taught us a lesson about the uncertainty of life and helped us to put our own lives into perspective. Death showed us what we valued most in life – very simply, our family relationships. My husband and I love one another and we both love our two boys dearly, but we regard every day that we all live normal happy lives as a precious gift.
>
> From time to time, we are still haunted by Tommy's memory, and I wonder if we will ever get over it completely. My husband still tends to withdraw when I need his strength

and comfort, but I guess it takes a long time to change a life-long habit.

In addition, parents should refrain from making any impulsive decisions about their lifestyle. A decision to change careers or to move to another house should be weighed very, very carefully. There is always pain and sadness when a child dies, but impulsive changes will not lessen the emotion. Change, like fantasizing, may appear to bring temporary relief, but will not offer any long term satisfaction. After a while, when the healing has begun, and when families have had time to think about restructuring their lives, changes can still be made.

The family which has endured the death of a child has lost a part of itself which can never be replaced, and it has forfeited a stake in the future which will never be repeated. It is devastating to be forced to say goodbye to a child whom one is just starting to know and love and whose very existence is based on an inherent faith in the future and on a desire to perpetuate one's own hopes and ideals. The death of a child shatters vanity and illusion and it reveals, to anyone who has experienced it, the incredibly fragile and precious thread upon which life and death are balanced – for facing death is really facing life.

III
DEATH IN ADOLESCENCE

The adolescent years represent a time of becoming, of changing and of separating, of testing and of learning. They are years filled with an incredible energy and vitality for every aspect of life. Physical development is almost complete, vocational choices are being formulated and independence beyond the family setting is beginning to occur. It is a time of great intensity, of insecurity alternating with self-reliance, shyness alternating with brashness, of isolation alternating with conformity, of peer values alternating with parental advice.

Between the disciplined freedom of childhood and the weighty responsibilities of adult life, the adolescent years provide the time to test oneself and to experiment with life. Crises take on a significance beyond realistic proportions and wild swings of mood are common. Major disappointments in life and in love have likely not been encountered in the adolescent years and a general feeling of optimism prevails. The typical teenager is preoccupied with career selection and with establishing a sense of self and a mature sexual identity.

It is difficult to imagine that some adolescents die during this critical stage in their lives. Some die in accidents or by suicide; most of the others die after a struggle with cancer. Sometimes families have time to prepare themselves for losing their teenager, but often there is no warning at all.

Accidents can happen at any time to anyone and there is virtually nothing families can do to anticipate the shock of hearing that their teenager has been accidentally killed. It is a senseless and devastating shock for which no justification whatsoever can be found. A family may take years to recover from the loss.

Sometimes teenagers commit suicide and a family is faced not only with a terrible kind of death but with the added burden of humiliation and responsibility. Many families simply refuse to believe that their teenager has killed himself and dissipate a great deal of energy, not in grief, but in denial. They often conceal the pain of reality behind the facade of an accidental death or foul play. One couple, whose 18-year-old son jumped in front of the subway and was instantly killed, insisted that he had, in fact, fainted. They persisted with the story despite the fact that eyewitnesses confirmed the suicide. At the same time they completely blocked out the knowledge that he had been severely depressed for several months and had become more and more withdrawn during the days preceding the suicide. This couple's reaction, although not unusual, is not a healthy one in the long term. Never admitting publicly that their son had killed himself demonstrated a denial of all of the family's problems. In reality, both parents knew the truth and blamed themselves. Their denial has magnified their problems to the extent that the mother has become an alcoholic and the father is suffering from a great deal of anxiety. Neither has made any attempt to deal with either the truth or with the burden of responsibility which both parents share.

There is another aspect of teenage death which is neither painless nor planned, but which saps the vitality of the victim and turns his dying into a lengthy and arduous battle with the very fabric of adolescence. Some teenagers die of cancer, which must surely be the most painful thing that a parent must ever tell a stricken son or daughter. Cancer does not necessarily mean a rapid death for an adolescent. Improved surgical techniques and chemotherapy can considerably lengthen the period of remission and many are still alive years after the initial diagnosis. Certainly they have every right to know about their disease and every right to be resentful if they are not kept

completely informed. This is difficult for parents who may be
more realistic about the disease than their offspring and who
often blame themselves for ignoring the symptoms and delay-
ing treatment.

For the teenager stricken with cancer, however, the concern is less with death than with life. The teenager who is
overwhelmingly concerned about becoming an adult, about
bodily changes and about appearance, absolutely despises
treatments which alter his or her appearance. When hair falls
out after chemotherapy, when scars are visible after surgery,
and when weakness and weight loss occur after treatments,
adolescents become acutely aware of being different, not only
from their friends but also from their previously healthy state.
They are terribly worried about mutilation of their bodies and
equally distressed about the barrage of tests and sessions in
hospital. This is particularly true for young people who may
have had no previous hospital experience at all. Their concern,
almost until the time of dying, is not with death, but rather
with the quality of life.

Many teenagers want to continue leading as active a life as
possible when stricken with cancer and they can seem surprisingly well during periods of remission. One boy played champi-
onship hockey. This is not unusual. Many teenagers who are
stricken with cancer seem to involve themselves in a kind of
over-activity as if not wanting to let the cancer beat them and
as if trying to get as much as they can out of life. A nurse de-
scribes how treatments can be arranged:

> After the initial diagnosis is made we normally start
> teenagers on a course of treatments. We try to arrange the
> treatments so they can have as much time as possible out-
> side the hospital. If they are going to school we try to have
> them come in Friday to Sunday. This way there is as little
> disruption as possible in their lives.

The nurse also described a 15-year-old boy who had to
have his leg amputated:

> He walked a mile to school in the morning, home for

lunch, back to school and back home again at the end of the day. He wouldn't take a lunch to school because he didn't want to be different from the other boys. His stump was becoming very sore but he would put up with the pain. He couldn't run with the other boys when they were changing classes and that bothered him a lot. He tried so hard to do everything the other boys did because he didn't want to be singled out as being different.

Another girl who had her leg amputated relearned how to swim, ski, and scuba dive with only one leg. Some teenagers, who are determined to live as actively as possible and who get a lot of support from their families, really make the best of their problems and just don't give up.

Those at school or university will probably wish to continue their studies and should be encouraged to do so. There is often an increased desire for knowledge during a fatal illness and, while it is impossible to make any long-term plans, doctors usually advise such teenagers not to think about dying as long as they seem to be responding to treatment. Their illness may lead to death or it may lead to life. While it may be difficult to be optimistic there is little value in being unduly pessimistic.

Karen described her fight with cancer in this way:

Last summer my leg started to get sore. I was 18 at the time. I went to the doctor and he thought it was my muscles. It started to get worse and really hurt after I was on my feet for a while. My family doctor thought he should have the leg X-rayed. They did special types of X-rays which took a long time and I had to go into the hospital overnight for tests. I guess they knew at that time what I had but they didn't tell me. I didn't really know what was happening until they brought me to this hospital which is 200 miles from my home and then I knew it must be something. I had a biopsy done and they told me right after that it was cancer.

When the doctor told me, he first asked me if I had any idea what it could be. I said no, even though deep down I thought the worst. When I found out the truth it wasn't that bad for me – I guess. I was kind of upset, but it wasn't that bad for me. My parents were both upset about it, but my Mom was worse. She worries so much. My Mom told my fourteen year old sister but when I came home she never said anything to me, so I don't really know what her reaction was. I found that sort of weird. People were afraid to ask me about it. At first I didn't want to tell any of my friends because I thought it would upset them too much. But then I realized there would be a change in me when I went home, so I'd better tell them beforehand so it wouldn't be such a shock. My friends were pretty upset and worried. I didn't have any problems with losing friends, but another girl I know here told me some of her friends didn't seem to be as close after she lost her leg. It helped me a lot to have my friends stick with me.

After the operation I had to stay in the hospital for a month of chemotherapy. Now I have to come in here for chemotherapy every three weeks. The treatments don't bother me anymore. At first I got pretty sick, I had a temperature and a bloody nose. I had to have a blood transfusion. My hands went numb too – that was really weird. I couldn't keep anything down, not liquid or anything, for a few weeks. I had to have intravenous feeding and I lost a lot of weight. But since then I didn't seem to get sick anymore.

The doctors were really good about explaining the treatments and answered any questions I had. They told me my hair would probably fall out, and it did. The biggest thing for me was losing my hair. I didn't have long hair, but some people have really long hair and it's really hard on them. They get you a wig, but anyone I know doesn't wear it because they just don't like it, it's not that comfortable. Most people just wear scarves. After the treatments any kind of food makes you really sick. Just the smell of food makes you nauseated.

When I was here in this hospital the first time, each day seemed like such a long time. It would drag on and on, and I'd still be here. It really hurt a lot after the operation, it was really sore. I could just lie on my back, I couldn't move that much. I still get these phantom pains. The brain doesn't know that the leg and foot aren't there and it still seems like they're there. You get these tingling sensations. You get them for a long time. I still get them now but they're not as bad. Before they used to be really bad. Before I had cancer I used to hate needles but now they don't bother me at all. You get used to the pain. You know you have to get needles, so what can you do?

I wear a prosthesis, but I still walk with a limp. I always wear slacks so people can't see it. Sometimes people ask me why I walk this way. I used to tell them truth, but it was such a shock to them, they wouldn't know what to say or do. They would just be stunned. Little kids aren't too bad. Sometimes when they ask you just say, "I was sick and I had to get help . . ." but the parents look at you and at their child in panic and say, "Don't say anymore," before you have a chance to explain what happened. The adults are more uptight about it than the kids. It doesn't bother me to talk about my cancer, but the reactions of people are too much. So when they say, "Did you twist your leg?" I just say, "Yes." I won't go into it anymore.

I walk with a cane now, and get around pretty well. I go shopping and do just about anything I did before. In my therapy at the hospital I play badminton, volleyball, and bowling. I tried riding a bike and that's not too bad either.

Karen has accepted her cancer and the loss of her leg remarkably well. She does not think about the future much because thinking about the future entails wondering about what life will be like, and when death will come. It is typical of teenagers with cancer that they live for today.

I don't think much about the future. Probably next year I'll go to school but I'm not sure. I was always one of these people who never really knew what they wanted to do. I thought something with helping people, but not a nurse. I don't think I could do that. You get too attached to people, and if something happens – you know – I get too emotional and I don't think I could handle it. Around here there were at few people who died in a short while, and that was really hard to take. It would be hard for me to be detached. After all you see these people all the time, I couldn't take it.

There are, however, many ways in which teenagers can react to a potentially fatal illness. Some go out of their way to protect their families by keeping their pain and fears to themselves. One boy, at the end of his first remission, confided his fears about dying to a close friend, but would not talk to his family for fear of worrying them. Parents should, of course, be encouraged to talk – fears which are exposed are much easier to overcome.

Some teenagers become exceedingly generous and more concerned about the members of their families than themselves. One 14-year-old girl, Joanne, who was close to death, was very upset when she found out her mother was pregnant. Joanne was so weak that she had to be carried and lifted as she did not have the strength to get around on her own. Her mother was caring for her at home and was lifting her several times a day. Joanne found out that her mother was not supposed to be lifting anything heavy during her pregnancy and was terribly upset by her mother's disregard for this advice. She refused to let her mother care for her at home any longer and was transferred to a hospital where she died two weeks later. This girl was more concerned with her mother's health than with her own. She was unselfish all her life, and even at her death.

Another girl was making a blanket to leave behind for her brother when she died. Her wish was to leave something tangible which would remain as her contact with her brother. She felt that each time he wrapped himself in the blanket he would remember her with warm feelings, and that would be their link.

Some teenagers are afraid that their deaths will create problems because they feel they are needed in the family. One young girl who was dying was very upset about leaving her father alone. Her mother had died two years earlier and she had been taking care of the household ever since. She felt she was now abandoning her father as well and that her death would leave the house and family in turmoil again.

These moods can change quickly, however, and generosity can quickly turn to bitterness, anger and depression over the disease which has attacked them. It is often interesting to consider how professional caregivers react to teenagers with cancer as they have an opportunity to view the patients by themselves and also while interacting with their families. Nurses in particular have valuable insights into the emotions experienced by young cancer victims and by parents who are often reluctant to believe that a member of the family has actually been stricken.

Miss L., a nurse, said:

We talk to the kids about their disease and try to cheer them up. Sometimes they are willing to talk, sometimes they aren't. If they are feeling well, why should they dwell on it? There is nothing wrong with healthy denial, we all do it. Sometimes they get depressed and then they just curl up for an hour or two, but when they feel better they bounce right back. Some teenagers get more depressed than others. We had two 15-year-old boys who both came in around the same time with the same type of cancer, although the prognosis was different in each case. One boy died quite rapidly and the other one naturally became very distressed. All he does now is sit around. He won't talk much and doesn't do anything active. He hasn't been able to get over the death as yet because of course he sees himself in the same position. What we try to tell him is that each case is different, and not everyone's disease progresses the same way, but for the moment he has lost all hope. It's very sad.

For the parents of a teenager stricken with cancer the role is an exceedingly precarious one. Mood changes, uncertainty about the future, and preoccupation with hospitals and illness can make coping with a sick teenager a difficult and sometimes perplexing task. Although parents must try to be as supportive as possible they must also avoid yielding to the demands of a sick child. Often gifts are lavished on a sick son or daughter as if to somehow compensate for the illness. As one boy said, "I must be going to die. I've been asking for a new stereo for years, and suddenly now I get it." A sick teenager may also be receiving extra and sometimes excessive amounts of attention from parents:

> I always tell mothers to share their time with all of their children. We can look after their teenagers in the morning so they can spend lunchtime with their other children. I think it's important that the mother doesn't forget the rest of the family.

It is important to organize time so that all members of the family can share equally.

When a cancer-stricken son or daughter no longer responds to treatment parents become afraid and this often increases the patient's general anxiety. Many parents do not want to care for their teenager at home simply because they are so frightened of the actual moment of death. As a result most teenagers die in hospital. No family is unique in this fear: it results from a dread of the unknown and the expectation that the actual death will be a dramatic and horrifying moment. It is usually quite the contrary – often an extension of a semi-conscious state in which the actual moment of death is almost impossible to pinpoint.

Miss L., as a nurse, also provides invaluable support for both the patient and the family when death is near:

> When a teenager is finally dying the parents are really afraid. They need someone to be with them. I may sit in the room with the parents and just talk to them for a few minutes. Sometimes when patients are unconscious I sit down and hold their hands for a while. Even though they are unconscious they somehow sense you are there with them. I think all dying kids are special, and I try to ensure they are not alone. Our job is to relieve their pain and be with them. Some don't even want to talk: they just want you to be with them because they are so afraid of dying alone.
>
> Some of our teenagers are so brave. An 18-year-old boy on the ward was paralyzed from the waist down. He had been

very athletic up until the time he got sick. I asked him whether he felt badly that he couldn't move around anymore. He answered, that it is like a car: first it runs alright, then it breaks down and you patch it and patch it. Eventually there comes a time when you can't patch it anymore and it just stops. He said he had now reached that time himself.

The death of one's teenager is more than the death of a hope or a dream as is the case with an infant or small child. The death of a teenager represents the death of a child whose parents know exactly what they are losing. It is probably too late to become pregnant again or to consider adoption. The death of a teenager is a terrible tragedy – it is an irreplaceable and unforgettable loss for a family to endure.

Susan, who was nineteen years old when she died from Ewings Disease, a form of bone cancer, had done a great deal of thinking about life and about her illness. After Susan died her mother agreed to allow publication of an essay written by her daughter:

All through my life I've been told that the greatest fear man must face in his life is the fear of the unknown or the uncertain. When I was younger I imagined the unknown as a dark mysterious cave, containing all sorts of terrible and ferocious creatures. Later I become more philosophical, and was confronted with the usual thoughts of death and what the situation after death was going to be like. I guess everyone's conception of the unknown changes with time, but mine took its final transformation, not because I suddenly was older and wiser, but because at the age of eighteen I developed cancer. When I first learned of my malignancy I faced the cancer with strength and courage. The disease had badly damaged my right leg and my walking was greatly impaired. But I would not accept even a limp. I vowed that I would do again all the activities that I had once been able to do. Activities that I had taken so much for granted before. Suddenly the joys of swimming, riding a bicycle, and playing a game of tennis came flooding back to me. I longed for that feeling of freedom that one experiences when just running. I wanted, for the first time in my life when it was impossible for me to have it, I really wanted my mobility again.

I could only think why me? Why at my age? Why strike me now, at my prime? Why not wait forty years when I've had my chance to do my living? At this point in the illness I was kept unaware of the even darker side of the cancer that I had developed. I knew only of the immediate muscle damage that was responsible for my weakened condition and for the limp that haunted me.

To live the rest of my life with at best a physical disability seemed to me to be the highest form of cruelty. I was being teased. Something I had grown to love and cherish was being dangled in front of me, just beyond my grasp. I felt robbed and cheated. And I was so angry at myself for not having used my life better. The time when I had my health was so precious, and I hadn't realized it. Of course, no one ever does. No one counts his or her health as a blessing until after that good health is gone.

When I was released from the hospital and was able to be up and around the house my fears were overpowering at first. Because of the extreme weakness in my legs I was afraid that when I tried to stand up I would fall to the floor. One day I went outside and insisted that I have one person on either side of me. I had lost over forty pounds (from 110 to 65) and I truly feared that I would be blown down by the wind. I lived in constant fear of hurting myself.

I also suffered from depression. The few things that I was able to do for myself gave me no joy or feeling of accomplishment. For a girl who rode miles on her bike and swam lengths of the front crawl it was difficult to accept the fact that now I was too weak to spray my underarms with deodorant. I needed such a great deal of help from my mother that I began to think of myself as a burden. I couldn't make myself a cup of coffee because the kettle was too heavy to lift. This dependency bothered me. I was 18 years old and afraid to be left alone.

I continued to exercise my right leg as my strength permitted. A long walk for me was made up of about four house lots, always keeping in mind that I had the same distance to go back again. By this time I had lost all sense of what distances healthy people could walk, and with what speed. I fooled myself into thinking that I was well within reach of that state of health which I looked upon with envy – normal. When I went anywhere in the car with my family I would watch healthy young people at crosswalks and wonder if they were even aware of the precious ability they possessed.

Then came the shocking news that my cancer had started up again, this time in a new place, my lungs. I can certainly say that when I knew of the recurrence I was at the lowest point anyone can reach. All my faith was gone. All my will to fight was gone. I was totally devastated.

I again went into hospital, this time one which specialized in cancer. I found myself on the children's ward with children my own age and younger, some of them much, much younger. Up until now I had considered cancer an illness that only struck older people, an idea that greatly contributed to my earlier feeling that I had been robbed of many years of happiness. Now I faced children, some only months old, who suffered from the same killer as I did.

I also learned more about my own type of cancer, both by observing others with it and by questioning the doctors for concrete answers. I learned that my tumour keeps coming back again, and again, and again. Although I respond well to radiation, powerful rays capable of killing cells in their path and to chemotherapy, drugs injected into the bloodstream, travelling to every part of your body, there is still the strong possibility that all the malignant cells have not been killed.

These two forms of treatment, radiation, and chemotherapy, are not foolproof, which is difficult to accept. But what makes it even harder on the patient is that the side effects of the treatment are so horrible. You become so ill, yet you have no guarantee that the treatment will make you well again. The most common side effects, nausea and baldness, would be hard enough to take in stride even if you knew that they were necessary for you to eventually become well. But there is no guarantee. And hence there is no comfort. The uncertainty that I must live with daily is almost unbearable.

But now that I know the truth about my cancer I try very hard not to think about it. I've experienced the one recurrence, and I think that I'll be able to handle any more recurrences, if they should occur. Now my days are spent in concentration on the good aspects of my life. And some good has come out of this terrible illness. I think that I've finally sorted out what, at least for me, is important in life.

I'm not so concerned anymore about that limp which bothered me all those months. And maybe having no hair has something to do with sorting things out in your life. I'm not worried about the current styles or what shampoo to use for my type of hair.

This illness has removed all the trivialities that fill a normal person's life. My life is not influenced by external pressures. I don't have to be at work at a certain time. I don't have to get along with a boss whom I really dislike, and I don't have to worry about having the right change to save time and patience when I buy tickets on the bus.

It comes down to a question of priorities, and I don't have a very long list. It's a pretty basic one too, because I'm down to the basics of life – living and dying. I want to live the best way I know how, and I want to be as happy as I can possibly be. And I want those close to me to be happy too.

My day is filled with the things that will bring me the closest to my goals. And what I can do, I will do, because I don't know what the future holds for me. In a few months I may be paralyzed, or even dead. But I don't worry about that now. I just thank God every morning that I am able to walk, and I do walk.

I may be limited in the things I can do, but I make sure that everything that I'm capable of doing, I do. I will never again say that I wish I had done something when I was able to do it. Now I take the opportunities as they are presented. If I wasted them I would never forgive myself. And that feeling of having wasted something precious is more terrible to live with than the fear of the unknown.

Susan desperately wanted to live long enough to see one of her sisters who was on an overseas trip, but just couldn't wait any longer. She died within a few days of completing her composition.

There are innumerable things that families can do for themselves and for their dying teenagers to ease the anxiety which surrounds the illness and death. A family whose teenager is faced with a diagnosis of cancer should give itself time and space to think for a few days before facing the outside world. It is important to sift out one's own most pressing emotions from the initial panic and disbelief before facing grandparents and other friends and relatives. Many close relatives will express disbelief, insist that the doctor has made an error and suggest that a "better doctor" should be consulted. It is important that parents be prepared for this kind of denial so that they are not faced with having to argue that their son or daughter does, in fact, have cancer or some other illness.

There should, of course, be no secrets from the adolescent who is ill. It is impossible to have any secrets in a situation such as this in any case, and any attempt to suppress information only compounds the existing anxiety. In addition, hiding the truth prevents parents from having a good relationship with their son or daughter at precisely the time when this relationship is so critical. This is very often a time when parents, because of time commitments, become closer to their teenager than ever before. The sadness is in the pain that is experienced by a parent who really comes to know a child only when it is too late.

For the teenager in hospital, a book, a portable radio or tape recorder, or a favourite meal prepared and brought in, are often appreciated. It is important, however, to avoid becoming over-indulgent and if the adolescent's behaviour patterns deteriorate they must be dealt with immediately. It is often a great comfort for the entire family to have a dying teenager cared for at home. Brothers and sisters feel useful and families who care for their dying very often find it easier to cope with their sadness after the death.

Fatally ill teenagers must be encouraged to live each day as fully as possible and to do and say all the things they want to. Most teenagers will probably want to continue in a familiar life pattern. However, some may want to try new foods, a new sport or do some travelling. If time and money are available, such wishes should be accommodated. Some may wish to discuss donating an organ, contributing to a research agency or planning a particular kind of funeral. It is essential for the dying adolescent to feel free and to be encouraged to discuss any of these topics, no matter how sad the feelings. It is also important to realize that many teenagers now live for years with cancers which used to be fatal in months. Not only are survival rates improving, but the quality of life for the survivor is improving as well.

To die as an adolescent is to die in the spring of one's lifetime. Michael, who wrote the following poem about life and death, died of cancer at age twelve.

What Do Seasons Mean?
Winter is a time of thought,
A time of stillness, quietness, loneliness,
A time of peaceful tranquility,
A time to think of what had not long ago preceded this
    time.

Autumn, perhaps a gift of God to prepare us for death.
But death, what does death hold?
Who knows death?
No one knows but we see it all around us.
The trees, the flowers, weeds, the people,
We all must die.
But death, who knows death?
Autumn knows death.
But does Autumn know life?

No, Spring knows life.
A time of resurrection,
Resurrection from the dead.
But what is Resurrection?

Resurrection is to be risen from the dead of life.
Life is God's promise.

Michael Clarke, age 11

IV
WHEN A PARENT DIES

How Children React to a Parent's Death

The loss of a parent is one of the most painful experiences in childhood, and despite the passing of time, it is impossible to forget a beloved parent. At each important event, on birthdays, at graduations and weddings, the beloved dead parent will be remembered and missed. Losing a parent leaves a lifelong mark on a child and even if the death is accepted, the loss will never be forgotten.

Surviving parents are often interested to know that a child's age is a major factor in how he or she will cope with the death of a parent. As children become older they will begin to expand their relationships, but young children are loved only by their parents, and love only them. The younger the children, the more they depend on their parents, especially on their mothers, for loving, feeding, cleaning and clothing. If a mother dies when she has infants or toddlers at home, and if the children's emotional and physical needs are not met as before, her death may have a very serious impact on their lives.

During the first two years of life children do not know what death is. Infants and very young children cannot tell the difference between death and any other reason that the parent is away; their reaction is the same to both. They begin to understand the meaning of death very gradually after the age of two. By that time, children will have seen dead insects or animals and, with adult guidance, can learn about the meaning of death.

Toddlers of two or three who lose a parent, especially

their mother, may be too young to express their feelings. Even at the age of six or seven, many don't understand death. Because they felt so close to their mothers they can't differentiate their fate from hers. Sometimes young children will convey their sadness at separation by curtailing their walking or talking or by losing bladder control. Some may get sick or lose their appetites and all interest in their surroundings. Since they can't express themselves adequately in words, they communicate the only way they know how – physically. At that age they depend heavily on their mother for encouragement and reward of physical achievements such as walking and talking. With mother gone they may lose interest in doing well. Here is one family's example:

Two and a half-year-old Cindy was beginning to talk very well, and had an excellent vocabulary for a child of her age. When her mother died, she gradually started to revert back to baby talk. It was only after her father recognized the problem and talked to Cindy that things started to get better. He took time to explain exactly what had happened to her mother, and encouraged her to tell him how she felt. He praised her use of language, and encouraged her to verbalize her feelings as much as possible. Cindy's speech gradually improved again as she and her father shared their sadness with each other. This is a good example of how important the surviving parent is to his or her children. Without this father's careful attention to Cindy's problem she might have suffered much more than she did.

It is not unusual for young children to become very active after the death of a parent because they fear death themselves. If they have a primitive understanding of what death is they might only know that dead bodies are stiff and do not move. Just to differentiate themselves from the dead, they run, jump, scream, and do anything to keep moving and prove to themselves and the world that they are alive.

If a child has experienced the loss of a parent between the ages of three and five, that child will probably view death as a

process which can be reversed. At this stage they may acknowledge that their father or mother is dead but also ask
when he or she is coming home again. At this age they can
express feelings verbally but they need parental support and
encouragement to do so. They worry about how the death has
happened, what will happen to the body, and whether they too
will die. It is very important that the surviving parent be
aware of all these concerns and reassure such children that
they will not die. Naturally, another of their major concerns
will be whether or not they will be taken care of as before,
because they are too young to look after themselves. If another
woman comes in to the home to take care of them it is only
natural that they will begin comparing her with the dead
mother.

From about the age of five onward children begin to have
a more realistic notion of death and understand that it is irre-
versible and inevitable. However many have trouble seeing
death as a bodily process. Instead they see it as a person, a
death-man or skeleton, who takes people away. By the age of
ten most children have abandoned the death-man idea, and
see death as it really is – the termination of life.

Another factor in how children cope with death of a parent
is related to the personality and disposition of the child. If they
allow themselves to feel the pain and the rage they will recover much more quickly than those children who cannot express their feelings. They also take cues from the surviving
parent and other members of the family. Children who see
people crying openly will feel encouraged to do the same.

The cause of death will also affect children's reactions to
it. If their father was driving a car, and the children distracted
his attention, causing him to have a fatal accident, they could
feel guilty for the rest of their lives. Their mother must assume the task of comforting them and telling them the death
was not their fault. If, on the other hand, the husband died of
cancer, and the children understood that they had nothing to
do with the disease and would not fall victim to it themselves,
they would probably cope much better.

Another factor affecting how children get over a parent's death is the amount of support they receive from the surviving parent. If a wife and mother dies it is important that the children witness the despair which results. It will encourage them to express their own grief. On the other hand, if the father keeps a stiff upper lip and only cries in the privacy of his own room, if at all, the children might think it is wrong to express their pain and will keep it stored inside. Before people can get over the loss of a loved one they have to go through a period of mourning. During this time they spend a lot of time thinking about the dead person and what the loss will mean to them. It is only after they have experienced this pain of separation and their grief that they can start reinvesting their love and attention in living people.

At every age, losing a parent is a terrible blow for children. However, the older they get the less chance there is that the effects will be permanent or profound. Older children can cope with stress better. They can do things for themselves and are not totally dependent on their parents for care.

If the child has been very close to the parent who has died, he or she may unknowingly imitate that parent's behaviour in his or her own life. A daughter may take over her dead mother's role in the family by assuming all her duties, and even behaving as she did. One woman loved her father intensely when she was a child and took over his place in the family after his death, with very unhappy consequences. Jane's is such a case:

> I always felt that of the four children in our family, my father considered me special. He used to talk to me, and really spoil me by letting me do what I wanted. I admired him so much, and at times I thought he must be God and could do no wrong. I was sure there was a special bond between us. Suddenly, one day he died in a car accident, and I felt I had lost the most precious person in my life. I was only nine years old, but the memory of our relationship dominated my life for many years afterwards.
>
> When my father died no one talked about his death, and

we all went on as if he were still alive. The first day my mother came to us in a dreadful state. She was bad for one day, but after that she was fine and did not shed another tear. He was just gone from our lives, and I don't remember weeping or mourning for him. As children do, we followed our mother's example and did not express our grief at all.

After the death of her father, Jane took over his role in the family:

It was almost an unwritten fact that I would be the one who would stay to look after my mother. My grandmother even said to me. "Jenny will marry, but you'll stay with your mother."

It was the worst thing Jane could have done because her mother was a very domineering woman and expected perfection from her family. Needless to say, that is an impossible standard to live up to. Apparently her father had been very different. He was more lenient and a much softer person than his wife.

Jane had trouble accepting the fact that her father was dead because her family acted as if he were still with them. As a result, her ties to her father remained as strong as ever:

I guess no one ever really accepted the fact that my father was dead and gone. My family, being Irish, had some of the renowned Irish magic in it. I remember one night, my uncle, grandmother, and mother were all sitting around the kitchen table. Suddenly my uncle got up, went to the door, opened it and listened for a moment, then closed it again. He went over to my mother, nodded to her and said, "Yes, it was him." They maintained that it was my father they had heard going up the stairs.

With her father not around to indulge her, Jane lost her favoured position in the family and began to encounter psychological problems. She lost a lot of weight and started having trouble at school. Her most serious problem, though, was her inability to relate to other people, especially men:

When I was growing up, I always felt I was different from

other people. I felt there was something wrong with me, but I couldn't quite explain it to myself. I used to think about my father a lot, and really he was the only man in my life. I remembered that as a child he talked to me, and when I was young he held me, and it was very comforting to be with him. I felt very tied to him, and even acted like him in many ways. He had been a lab technician, so naturally I became one too.

I ran into problems in my early twenties because although I liked men, I had tremendous difficulties in relating to them. There was one man I was attracted to in my bad-minton club, but I didn't know how to act in his company. He was a journalist and a very nice chap, but I froze when I was with him, despite my feelings for him.

One night he said to me, "The moving finger writes, and having written moves on." He never bothered again – that was the end. That was when I had my first breakdown. I started weeping and having periods of depression after-wards. I could weep at any time, and my mother used to say to me, "You'll be old looking by the time you're thirty if you keep on weeping." I always said to myself at those times, if my father had lived I would have been fine.

I used to see him so vividly in my mind and my dreams, and I still see him clearly now, more than thirty years later. Sometimes I have nightmares about him. I had one horri-ble one recently where he was sitting on top of his tomb-stone, with no eyes. I can't seem to escape from my memo-ries of him – I wish I could forget him. I sometimes think I was hypnotized at a certain stage of my development, and just stuck there, still involved with my father.

Looking back now I can see that the relationship I had with my father was too close to have been a healthy one. I feel I have lost so many years of my life being tied to a dead man. Because I was so involved with him there was no room for any other men in my life, and I guess that is why I have never married. I stayed at home with my mother until I was thirty, when I was advised by a minister to get away. I'll never forget how he put it, "Jane, nothing grows under a spreading tree."

Jane left Ireland and moved to Canada where she has been living for sixteen years. Throughout her thirties, and now in her forties, she still has not been able to get close to a man:

> It's only since I have had psychotherapy that I realize he was very human like the rest of us, and had his faults which I would not or could not see before. But, I'm afraid it may be too late for me – the best years of my life have been wasted on a fantasy.

Jane has been a depressed woman for many years, and has had an unhappy life because she could never resolve her feelings about her dead father. She felt that she was special to him, and that their relationship was unique. Unfortunately he died at a time when this feeling was very strong. Had he lived another five years or so or had her mother been more supportive, she no doubt would have been upset, but she would have rapidly outgrown her fantasy and become like any other adolescent with a healthy interest in the opposite sex. The last thing adolescents want is to be tied to a parent, because it is a time for them to try out their own wings.

Jane's mother used her as a crutch and never encouraged her to get out on her own. Jane took over her father's place in the family, staying with her mother for twenty-one years and caring for her. She filled the vacuum in the family that her father's death had created, and then could barely escape.

Because her mother had never openly expressed her sadness about the death, Jane followed her example and went on living with all the grief left inside her. The sadness doesn't go away, and in Jane's case it came out in her weeping spells fifteen years later. She had never said goodbye to her father.

Since her psychotherapy Jane has not been so depressed about herself. Although she has not married, she spends more time with other people and is not as painfully shy as she was. She bought a condominium for herself and lives a quiet but lonely life.

How Adolescents React to a Parent's Death

Although death is always terrifying, it is much easier for a teenager to cope with a parent's death than it is for younger children. Adolescence is a time of growth and experimentation and along with that comes feelings of independence and self reliance. Of course, not all adolescents are the same, and some do continue to cling to their parents if they have been overprotected and feel insecure about their ability to make it on their own. In general, adolescents will be able to get over a parent's death more easily because parents aren't the only people in their lives. Friends can give them some of the things parents normally give: advice, support and companionship. The adolescent's personality probably will not suffer permanent damage because he or she has matured sufficiently to cope with the crisis.

Adolescents need their parents for different reasons than children. After all, parents are still closer than anyone else and adolescents need intimacy and love as we all do. Even though they are actively trying new things and experimenting, they still like to know that they have roots, and a home that is available.

I knew one family where the mother was killed in a car accident. She left behind a husband and two boys aged fourteen and sixteen. The boys' first reaction was one of utter horror and shock at the injustice of the death. When the funeral was held, they still couldn't believe that their mother would never be coming home again. Many of the boys' school friends came to the funeral and their presence touched these bereaved teenagers very much. They felt reassured that no matter what happened their friends still cared about them.

After the funeral was over this family had to decide how it was going to restructure. Since the boys were both at school and the father was at work during the day they needed someone to help with the domestic chores. They solved the problem by hiring a part-time housekeeper, and all pitched in to do the work on her days off. In the first few weeks the boys missed their mother's presence very much. The house seemed empty without her laugh, the smell of her home-made cakes or her scolding when they left their beds unmade. They used to like to talk to her when they came home from school about things they thought their Dad would find silly. They talked to their mother for hours about what their friends were like, their insecurities in certain social situations or what it was about their teachers they liked or disliked. For a long time they missed that, but the boys were lucky enough to have each other.

As the months went by they began to adapt to their new lifestyle without a mother. They learned how to do many more things on their own such as cooking meals or replacing buttons. Although they suffered bereavement at a young age, they were not left with any permanent scars. These teenagers were old enough and emotionally strong enough when their mother died to separate from her and make their own way in life.

As children get older, and build their own lives, the death of a parent is not as traumatic as it would have been earlier. Adolescents are no longer dependent on parents to such a great extent, and their death is not a direct threat to their way of life. At any age, losing a loved one is painful, but if you have no one and nothing else, the death of a parent can be shattering. A physician I knew told me about a ninety-three year old patient who was dying in hospital. Her seventy-year-old daughter, who had lived at home all her life, came to him one day in tears pleading, "Doctor, please do everything you can to save my mother. Don't let her die, she's the only thing I have." In adult life, most people separate from their parents and make their own lives. However, some adults never cut the umbilical cord, which makes the death of a parent almost as traumatic for them as it would have been in childhood.

The Effects of Remarriage on The Family

If you have lost your husband or wife, there may come a time when you are ready to love again, and you can begin looking for a person who might be suitable as a new spouse. You may be introduced to someone by friends, or you may meet someone socially and develop a relationship. Children cannot do this, much as they may want to, when they are ready to welcome a new parent into their lives. They may encourage their father to remarry because they want a new mother, but cannot actively seek a new mother themselves.

Under the age of five or six your children are quite helpless in seeking new people to love. Older children can often find caring neighbours or the parents of friends who can fill some of their needs for a caring adult. It is easiest for adolescents because they have the opportunity to go out and make new relationships and acquaintances. An adult who befriends children can provide them with affection and guidance, but can never replace the dead mother's or father's love.

There is sometimes a problem with timing when a new parent enters the home. The surviving parent may decide that he or she is ready for remarriage, but the children might not yet be ready for a new parent. On the other hand, children may be begging for a new parent, but the parent may not be ready to love again. It is a very lucky family that reaches the same point at the same time, and can find someone to step in who will please everyone.

Being a stepmother or stepfather is one of the most difficult roles in the family. Inevitably, children will compare him or her to the dead parent and will notice the differences. A new parent brings back painful memories for the children, and may also evoke conflicts of loyalty. Some children feel that they cannot be true to their dead mother's memory and still love this new mother who has come into the home. It is difficult for a parent not to be guilty of the same thing and to constantly remind a new husband or wife about things as they were before. If those problems can be overcome, the joy of having a new, caring and loving parent is very great. For young children, it will assure them that they will be taken care of again; for older children it will help them get through all the stages of growing up and maturing with both a mother and father figure; and for adolescents it means a potentially good relationship with two adults who will help them through their teenage years.

One man I knew lost his wife as a result of stomach cancer. He had two teenagers at home with him, a girl of thirteen and a boy of fifteen. About a year and a half after the death this man met a woman and fell in love with her. Not knowing how his children would react, he did not rush into another marriage. Instead, he gave his son and daughter time to get to know this woman and learn to trust her. About a year later they announced their plans to be married and the teenagers were delighted. When their new mother moved into their home they all reaped the benefits of having a new woman to love and to be loved by. Of course, not all families are this lucky.

A step-parent has the potential to be the worst thing that ever happened to a family if he or she cannot get along with the children. Sometimes a step-parent may bring his or her own children into the family, and this is an even greater adjustment for the family. The surviving parent and the new spouse may decide to have children of their own. If these children are given preferential treatment the other children may become very bitter. It is essential that the surviving parent try to ensure that the new parent will bring harmony to the household, and not bitterness.

How to Cope With a Parent's Death

If you are a surviving parent, one of the first decisions you must make is when and how to tell your children about the death. If the death has been sudden you should tell the children immediately. If you do not tell them, someone else may, or they may suspect something themselves. If you hide the truth your children will lose their trust in you, and will doubt your honesty in the future. Don't confuse young children with complicated religious and philosophical concepts about death, but explain death as simply as possible and assure them that they probably won't die until they are very old. If you overload them with abstract theories about death they may become confused and frightened. Keep all explanations simple, and don't give any more details than the children ask for and can understand.

If the death has followed a lengthy illness, your children should have been prepared for it long before it occurred. Even young children are very sensitive to what is going on and pick up feelings around them. If a parent is dying of a disease, and you do not tell your children, they get enough clues to figure it out for themselves. Children are aware of their parents' behaviour, and if it changes, they pick it up very quickly. Rather than pretending, be honest with them and tell them what is really happening. If their father has cancer, explain to your children in very simple terms what the disease is. Tell them about the medical care he is receiving, but explain to them that some diseases are incurable.

Encourage them to do something kind for the sick parent so they won't feel completely helpless and lost. Help them select a present, paint a picture, or pick some flowers to give to the sick parent, to express their love and affection. Telling your children that their parent is going to die is an awful thing to have to do - - it is probably one of the worst times your family will experience, but one that you must go through together.

If you take your children to the funeral, stay close to them. Hold them by the hand and give them strength: they will be able to cope with it if you can. Children take their cues from their parents: if you cry, they will feel its alright to cry. If you can bear the grief at the funeral, they will bear it as well. If you do not cry or show any signs of emotion, the children might feel it is wrong to cry and may keep their sadness pent up inside. Encourage the children to talk and show their pain. If they don't get it out they may develop serious personality problems later in life. Hidden grief never goes away, it just changes its form.

It will be much easier for children to get over the death if life goes on as before with no extra disruptions in routines. If you remain in the same house your children will be much happier. The last thing they want is to change homes, schools, and friends. After the funeral life must go on for the rest of the family, and it is much easier if the disruptions are kept minimal.

If your wife has died, and you have an infant or a young toddler at home, be certain to hire a good substitute mother to care for the child. At that age children are beginning to get close to their mothers; with the mother gone they need someone else who will be loving and caring. The younger the children the more important it is to have the same people around them. Too many changes in the people caring for them will upset them. When they are old enough to understand, perhaps at age three, tell them what happened to their real mother. Don't keep death a family secret. It is a terrible blow for a teenager to find out that the woman he thought was his real mother is really his stepmother. Children have a right to know the truth about their past.

If your children are older and go to school all day you might think of turning to extended family for help. You might expect their grandparents or aunts to offer to care for them. In some families this might be feasible, but in many it is too much to ask. Don't expect a grandmother to feel the same way about your child as your wife did. It's good to have extended family around for support but you may be disappointed if you expect too much from them.

If your husband has died, you and your children are left with a different set of problems. If you have not been working, you might be forced to find a job for economic reasons. If this happens, your children will have to make three adjustments – living without their father forever, losing their mother for part of the day, and a possible change in lifestyle because there is not as much money coming in. The important thing for children is to be sure they are well taken care of in this situation and don't feel abandoned. If you have preschool children, make sure they like the person caring for them. If they are at school and can look after themselves until you return from work, make sure you spend time with them in the evening, because they really need you then. Don't lose touch with your children. You are all they have left and they will look to you for mothering and fathering.

Don't use children as a crutch and expect them to take the place of their dead father: it's too much to ask of them. If their father was the dominant one in the family, try to take over his role yourself, but do not expect your son to become the man of the house. After the death of any member of the family, the whole family structure must be reorganized, and the duties and responsibilities reallocated. As the mother and the only surviving parent you must be prepared to take on many of the roles of the dead partner yourself.

If you have not experienced a death in the family you should prepare yourself for the remote possibility that you and your partner may die accidentally one day. Many couples never prepare for the possibility that they might be killed accidentally, leaving their children completely alone. All married couples should select a friend or relative to care for their children in the event of unforeseen tragedy. This should be thought over very carefully, and discussed with the people you have selected, and then it should be written into your will. This will ensure that your children will be looked after by people you have selected, and not by people who think they should step in.

The death of a parent places a tremendous stress on the family, and each person is affected in a different way. The best advice to the members of any family who have experienced such a loss is to stand by one another, because it is the time when you most need the family's support.

V
DEATH OF A GRANDPARENT

The Role of the Grandparent in the Family

Life as a grandparent has the potential to be very rewarding when people have worked out reasonable relationships with their families over the years. It provides an opportunity to pass on to the younger generations a tradition and legacy which have been important to you all your life. It is also a time when you can repair some of the problems of the past. You may never have had too much time to spend with your children because you were too busy working to make a living and now is the time you can make it up to them by having the time for your grandchildren. Your years as a grandparent can be happy ones, but they also have the potential to be very lonely and frustrating if your family isolates or rejects you.

As a grandparent, your grandchildren are very important to you. You do not have to face the day to day problems and frustrations of caring for them and can enjoy them for what they are without trying to change them. You can advise them on certain matters and give them the benefit of your experience. You have so much to give at that point of your life and your grandchildren seem the natural recipients.

As you grow older and retire, you will have more free time to spend with the family. You may find that your children and grandchildren become increasingly important to you as your own friends start dying one by one. Your focus shifts away from concern about yourself and what you will do the rest of your life. Instead you worry about the successes and happiness of the younger generation. They are your stake in the future

– you live on through your grandchildren. The continuity of the generations gives you hope.

As a member of the older generation, you could be a valuable person to your family. You have experienced many things in life and have gained insights which could make you an excellent kind of senior advisor. For example if you have been in business all your life, you will be able to help your children and grandchildren with any of their business problems. As a grandparent you can derive a great deal of pleasure from being an advisor without the responsibility of getting involved in the problem.

In some societies old people are venerated and looked upon as a source of wisdom. In our western culture, with its focus on youth, we have tended to neglect and isolate our old people. Many families do not respect age and experience and do not give competent and intelligent grandparents their rightful place in the family. Of course not all grandparents are wise and benevolent just because they are old. If people are mean and stubborn throughout their lives, they will be the same way in old age. However, for people who have led productive and successful lives, retirement should not be viewed as the gate to senility.

Families should recognize that such grandparents still have a lot to offer, and not cast them aside because they are old.

What You Pass On From Generation To Generation

As a grandparent you leave your children and grandchildren with a legacy consisting of many things. Initially you leave behind your biology which you have, in turn, inherited. They will inherit your looks, susceptibility to certain diseases, body structure and so on. You will also pass on religion and nationality as part of your legacy. When people die they leave behind a material legacy: all their money and possessions may be left to their descendants. Finally, you will leave behind a legacy which is not as obvious, as it is left in your children's minds and hearts. You leave for them a set of precedents and expectations which determine how they will live their lives in the present and in the future, and they, in turn, pass this on to their children as the generations evolve.

We have all heard the expression blood is thicker than water. You can choose your friends and if you grow apart you can always find new friends. It doesn't work that way with families. Family relationships go on and on. You cannot break them by becoming angry or leaving. Your mother is always your mother and whether you choose to live by her side or separated by a continent she still influences your life.

As parents you raise your children and instill in them values and a set of standards which were once instilled in you and by which you hope they will abide. All those childhood years spent with you create loyalties in your children's minds that they may not even be aware of. In return for everything you have given them, your children pass on to their children what you have taught them. However, it doesn't always work that way. If a man is angry with his parents for the way in which he was raised he may reject his parents' values and adopt an entirely different way of living. However, by doing this he is still influenced by his parents, although in a negative way.

Parents pass on not only good values and high morals to their children, they also pass on injustices, prejudices and psychological problems. We get both good and bad legacies and pass the same on to our children. One woman, Miss M., was having sexual problems which she could not seem to overcome. While digging back into the previous generations it turned out that her mother and grandmother had both been frigid. The same attitude toward sex and men had been subtly passed on from mother to daughter without ever having been made explicit. In any generation it is possible to unbalance the system and begin to pass on a negative trait. On the other hand, in any generation it is also possible to repair the problem, but that takes a lot of work and understanding. Eventually, through family therapy, this woman began to understand why her grandmother had first developed the problem. Many years back, as a young girl, she had a bad experience with an uncle who molested her and she was never able to respond to men after that time. She did marry and have a daughter, but her marriage broke up partly because of her negative feeling toward men. Her daughter, Miss M.'s mother, was also suffering from the same problem. She too married and had two children, but she had never enjoyed sex. Once she understood the whole scenario she was able to focus on her own problem. Eventually, after a great deal of hard work, she was able to develop a healthy interest in men.

Families establish their own intricate ways of operating which outsiders may not be able to understand. For example, in a family where the mother and father have a terrible relationship, the son may become a juvenile delinquent. In this way the parents' minds are diverted from their own marital problems because their son has given them something else to worry about. Somehow, unwittingly, he has been pushed into this type of behaviour by his parents in order to keep the family together. If the parents did not have their attention diverted by their son's behaviour they would have to face their own empty lives. That might break the family apart, so the pattern is continued. Change is a difficult thing for any family to cope with, and therefore appropriate behaviour patterns are established to maintain the status quo at all costs.

As generation follows generation conflicts arise between loyalty to the previous generation and loyalty to the spouse or even friends. Certain events prove to be very demanding for families because they mean change and the rebalancing of loyalties. Even happy events may evoke tensions. When a new baby is born, suddenly the children become parents and parents become grandparents. The grandparents can no longer demand as much from their own children who now have new loyalties to their own child. When there is a marriage, children become husbands or wives and once again must divide their loyalties between their families of origin and their new partner. An unhappy event such as death in the family creates many shock waves in the family. Suddenly all relationships with that person are over, and all the unresolved problems the survivors had with that person become highlighted.

How the Death of a Grandparent Affects the Family

When a grandparent dies in the family, problems are created not only for their children, but also for their grandchildren. The books are closed, and there are no further opportunities for you to tell them all the things you may have wanted to say to them one day. It's very common for people to leave things unsaid and problems unresolved thinking that one day they will deal with them. When a grandparent dies, their children have to face not only the loss of a mother or father, but also the end of a very important relationship. The grandchildren then have to suffer the impact of their parents' grief in addition to their own personal grief at losing a grandparent.

It is a difficult time for the family because you must all adapt to the change brought about by the death. The closer you were to the dead grandparent the greater the sense of loss will be in the family. In one family, the grandmother had lived at very close quarters for a few years while the mother was busy working. Consequently the grandmother played a large role in raising young Sarah. Since the family was so closely knit, the death of the grandmother affected Sarah profoundly. She described how the family functioned before the death:

> From the time I was five years old we lived in a duplex: our family was downstairs and grandma was upstairs. Because my father needed her help, my mother became completely involved in the family business while my grandma was at home taking care of me. I could only see my mother in the evenings. My grandmother was the major woman figure in my life for a long time. She was the one who dealt with me: When I was bad she disciplined me, but at the same time I knew I was her special grandchild. I was totally devoted to her.

We used to spend Saturday nights together watching Perry Mason on T.V. It was like a party. She would have a bag of chips there and we always had a lot of fun. Her husband died when she was still quite young so our family was very important to her. She only had two children, my mother and my uncle, and in my family I was the only child. When I think back I guess I was as special to her as she was to me.

Sarah's grandmother was really the matriarch of the family and although she was a strong and controlling woman she was kind at the same time. Because she lost her husband at a young age and had two children to raise, she had to support the family. She became a successful businesswoman, but while she was working all those years she did not have enough time for her children. Now that she was no longer working she was trying to give Sarah what she never gave her daughter: time and attention. Through Sarah she hoped she could repair the damage done to her own family.

Even though she did not spend a lot of time with her own daughter the ties were still very strong. Sarah's mother was very dependent on her own mother and was used to being controlled and manipulated by her. The most dramatic example of this was the fact that they lived in the same duplex for eight years. However, the grandmother, having seen the mistakes she made with her own daughter, tried to be more benevolent with Sarah:

Life was very rosy until I was thirteen. Suddenly, to my horror, grandma developed a brain tumour. I went to visit her in the hospital, but it was too much for me. It was terribly shocking to see her with all sorts of tubes inside her. Her skin was a very strange colour and I guess I panicked. I couldn't go near her because I felt afraid. Once I got over the initial shock of seeing her like that, all I could think of was that she was being taken away from me. It was a pretty selfish attitude.

She got sicker and sicker and finally slipped into a coma. Around that time my uncle was writing his final exams for dentistry. When he got his results he went to see her at the hospital. One of those unexplainable medical phenomena occurred when he went into her room. Although she had been in the coma for three weeks, she became lucid for a few minutes – just long enough to find out he passed his exams.

She died shortly thereafter. It was as if she had been waiting to settle everything before she let go. She was an incredible woman. I found out later that when she first learned of her tumour, she arranged for a family burial plot with her grave being the first one. She was always in control, even of her death.

For Sarah, losing her grandmother was very painful since her grandmother had been as close to her as a real mother and she had a severe reaction to the death which stayed with her for many years. Sarah thought her life was over and that everything worthwhile had been taken away from her. This once happy young girl became morbidly depressed, thinking she would be bereaved for the rest of her life:

After my grandmother's death I felt consistently sick, although I'm sure most of it was psychosomatic. I became very bitchy at school and lost a few friends because I was insulting and very bitter. Looking back now, I guess I was trying to make the rest of the world pay for what happened to me.

My life changed drastically because I was no longer indulged. My parents who were depressed because business was not going well did not cater to me and expected me to start acting like an adult. I wasn't ready for that. I always felt that grandma was preparing me for adulthood in her own way, but she died before she had a chance to teach me what I needed to know. I never knew that the whole world didn't revolve around me, and that was a hard lesson to learn.

Sarah had never accepted herself as being average because all her life she was told how special she was. She simply could not adjust to the idea that she was ordinary.

In later years she developed problems in her relationships

with men because she could inevitably fall for men who would put her back on the pedestal. She tended to be attracted to older men who pampered her and took care of her. She was looking for a replacement for her grandmother, someone who would make all her decisions and look after her. After all, it is much easier to let someone take care of you than to actually take control of your own life.

At the time of her grandmother's death, Sarah was not really included in the family's grief. She was not taken to the funeral but was sent to her great aunt's house where she stayed for a week. Sarah's family, being Jewish, observed shivah after the death. This is a ritual where for seven days friends and family gather together in the home of the bereaved to mourn the loss. During this period of concentrated mourning prayers are said for the dead and the mourners and visitors spend time talking about the dead person. The shivah can have a great therapeutic value since it forces people to face the loss and to begin to grieve. Since Sarah was kept away she did not participate in this and had more trouble than her parents in saying goodbye to her grandmother. Sarah described what happened in later years this way:

Things improved between my mother and myself after grandma's death and we got to know each other for the first time. I have always been a dependent type of person, and I transferred all my dependency needs on her. Despite that, my grandmother still played a very active role in my life because I consciously tried to pattern my life according to her expectations.

Although she was dead, in my mind I knew what would have pleased her and what she would have wanted me to do. I became like her in many ways – I had internalized all her values and morals. In more superficial ways I had even adopted her taste and style.

When I began to date, I used to try to imagine whether my grandmother would have approved. Finally, when I was twenty-seven, I met a man and became engaged to him. One of the first things I did was to visit the cemetery where my grandmother was buried. It was the first time I had ever gone there, but somehow I felt compelled to go. It was as if I had to tell my grandmother about my fiancée and clear it with her. I'm not a believer in the supernatural, but I have always felt there has been a type of communication through the grave. I can sit for hours with a problem and think about her and get some sort of an answer. Maybe I will work it all out myself. I really don't know.

Sarah did not go through with the marriage because she realized that, although her fiancé was prepared to fill all her dependency needs and cater to her, she was not in love with him. She became very depressed when she broke the engagement wondering whether she would ever be able to find a man she could love.

It was at this time that she sought professional help. The root of her problem was that she had never been able to mourn the death of her beloved grandmother and break her dependency ties. After a couple of years of psychotherapy Sarah began to feel much better, and put the death in its proper perspective. Unfortunately, there was another shock in store for her:

Four months ago my mother began to display the same symptoms as my grandmother had exhibited. When she saw the doctor he told her she also had developed the same type of brain tumour. It was just awful – we were all very upset. There were all sorts of strange coincidences. They were both the same age, fifty-six, when they developed the tumour. It was located in the same side of the head.

My mother had quit smoking for three and a half years and started smoking again when her mother became sick. I quit smoking for three and a half years, and I'm now back at it. Apparently it's very coincidental that a mother and daughter should have the same disease because these brain tumours are not supposed to be hereditary. It makes me wonder if I'm next. It's almost as if I can't escape fate.

My grandmother had been a businesswoman in her thirties and forties, my mother became a businesswoman, and now my father wants me to come into the business with him. It's almost as if this career were predestined. I have a strong feeling that I too will die in my fifties because I'm the third generation woman in that blood line.

My mother is dying now and I'm afraid I will fall apart again. I've had fantasies that I will be unable to communicate with the world. Just when I was getting over my grandmother's death, this happened. The only comforting thing for me is the thought that maybe grandma is waiting for my mother. When I think of that it gives me strength.

Sarah will cope with her mother's death much better than she did with her grandmother's because she is an adult now. She is no longer as dependent as she was at age thirteen. Since she does not live with her parents, her mother's death will not affect her day to day routines. However, she still tends to be emotionally dependent on her family and that is what she will have to come to terms with after the death. This family clearly illustrates how a legacy is passed from one generation to another and the impact the death of a grandparent can have on the survivors' lives.

The Problems of Aging Grandparents

If you are a grandparent who is growing old you should not consider it as a problem as long as you are healthy. It is really just another stage in human development. Except for the reduced ability to do some of the physical activities you did before and the vulnerability to physical stresses, there is really nothing negative about growing old.

You may find your children and grandchildren referring to you as old, but what does that really mean? There are two ways to define old age. One is a legal one. In Canada you are entitled to receive old age pensions when you reach sixty-five. The other one is a very personal one. You are old when you consider yourself to be old. The attitude you will have about yourself depends on how healthy you feel, whether you have been forced into retirement and if you are socially isolated through the death of your spouse, friends or family. Most peo-

ple don't think of themselves as old unless they have experienced at least one of these three things. The calendar has very
little to do with it.

If you become sick you are less able to cope with the associated physical and emotional stresses when you are old. Even
a minor illness is more likely to kill a ninety-five-year-old man
than it is a seventy-five-year-old because adaptability diminishes with age. As we all know, the saddest part of growing old
is knowing that death is near. If you are eighty-five, even if you
have never been sick a day in your life, you know your years
are numbered. However, it is impossible to die of old age,
death must be a result of an illness or an accident. People don't
just wear out. If you haven't experienced illness it's hard to
think of yourself dying. Once you get a disease you will suddenly have a reminder of your own mortality.

How a Grandparent Copes on the Death of a Spouse

While your spouse is still alive you can look to him or her for
companionship, help in running the household and many
other things you need. When he or she dies you are left to your
own resources. If you are healthy and want to remain in the
same house or apartment as long as you are able to afford it
there is no problem. The problems arise if you become sick
and unable to look after yourself or if you find living alone too
lonely. Because you are lonely you may expect your children
and grandchildren to visit you as much as they can. Don't forget they have their own lives as you have yours. If they are too
busy to visit you as frequently as you would like, try not to be
angry at them: it does not mean they don't love you.

In order to prevent having your family as your only source
of pleasure you should consider participating in some new activities. Your family may be too preoccupied to worry about
your loneliness, and if you keep active you can handle it much
better. If you are over sixty you might want to join a senior
citizens' group. There are many such groups in existence

which plan many different activities for its members. They provide a good way of getting out of the house as well as a means of meeting other people like yourself who may be alone.

The real problems arise for you and your family if you become sick and can no longer look after yourself. In one family, no one wanted to look after the seventy-year-old grandmother after her heart attack. She was left in a weakened condition and needed to be cared for. Since she had two daughters, both of whom had room in their homes, she assumed she would be asked to live with one of them. The family had never discussed what would happen in the event that grandma became sick and when the time came no one was willing to take her in. This came as a shock to the sick grandmother because she felt abandoned. When she was placed in an old age home she died about six months later.

The two daughters suffered a lot of guilt when they made the decision to put their mother in the home. As children they were always told by their parents, "No matter what happens to you, remember you always have a home you can come back to." However, as the years passed and they had their own children, they did not want their mother living with them and interfering with their lives. Still, when they placed her in the home they felt guilty because their mother let it be known she felt very let down. Their guilt increased when she died because they thought, "If only we had known it would have been for such a short time, we would have happily looked after her."

The problems arose in this family because the grandmother and her daughters had never discussed what would happen in the event of unforeseen illness. If the older woman had known well in advance that moving in with her children would not be convenient for them she would not have been so upset when the time came to find accommodation. Some families have the opposite problem. When left with an aging grandparent who needs care they fight over who will take him or her. You may find a situation where two daughters are fighting over their father's attention all their lives. When he is left alone and needs help both sisters will fight over who get to look after him.

You must make your own decision about whether to look after an aging parent or grandparent in your home. In our society there are alternatives available: nursing homes, chronic care homes, and homes for the aged all providing care for people no longer able to care for themselves. In the past families looked after their aging members at home because there was nowhere else for them to go. If you feel having a parent or grandparent in your home will place too many stresses on your own family life, talk it over with him or her and find an alternative. There is no right or wrong advice on this issue. It is up to you and your family to decide for yourselves what is the best solution for everyone. If you foresee the situation possibly arising, talk it over in advance and make your decision in a calm moment.

Your widowed parent or grandparent may feel well enough to remain in his or her own home and this should be respected. Don't feel that just because people are old they must be institutionalized. Allow him or her to remain in familiar surroundings as long as possible. It has been shown that for old people a change of environment can prove to be very stressful. They are much happier in a place they know, with all their belongings around them. It takes them much longer to adapt to new surroundings than younger people and they can become depressed if the change is too sudden. Let your parent or grandparent make his or her own decision about remaining at home.

Coping With a Grandparent's Death

The death of your grandparent may be the first experience you have with losing someone close. If you did not live with your grandparent, the death will not affect your family's daily routines. If it was a paternal grandparent who died, your father will be most affected because he has lost a parent. At any age it is very sad to lose a parent, because the emotional ties are so deep-rooted. The death also reminds your father of his own mortality because he is now a member of the older generation and next in line. In this situation it will be your father who is most bereaved and you should do your best to comfort him.

If your grandparent lived in a different city, and was not in close contact with your parents, they may suffer a lot of guilt when the grandparent dies. They may feel that they did not do enough for him or her or may regret how isolated they allowed the grandparent to become in later years. It is also more difficult for people to cope with the death of someone close if they feel guilty about how they treated the deceased before the death. If your parents lived in the same city as your grandparent and did everything they could for him or her, they may feel free to grieve without regretting the past.

As a grandchild, the more you saw your grandparent and the closer you were, the greater will be your sense of loss. If you barely knew your grandparents because they lived in another city, their death will not affect you that deeply. As with any other relationship, the greater a role the deceased played in your life, the more you will miss that person.

VI
A PARENT'S LEGACY

In the previous chapters, the painful and sometimes devastating effects of death within the family structure are detailed. Whether the death is that of an infant, a teenager, or of an elderly grandparent, there are, almost always, survivors who must experience the process of grief and then healing. Obviously, the survivors of a teenage suicide and the children of an elderly parent who dies after a lengthy illness will experience different kinds of loneliness, guilt and anger. But the process of grieving is inevitable if the survivors are to rebuild their lives and accept their own mortality.

Hopefully, as children grow older their dependence on their parents diminishes. Certainly, in North American society, the whole process of becoming an adult means strengthening one's independence from parental bonds, exploring and testing personal preferences and, in most cases, achieving the ability to function alone. Regardless of their relationship in life, those who survive the death of a parent are profoundly affected. Not only are they faced with the death of their first source of love and stability, but they are also struck by the knowledge that they themselves are no longer children, and that a relationship which may have existed for fifty or sixty years is over. The child has suddenly become the adult and must begin to accept the reality of human mortality.

Sometimes, it is not until the actual funeral that the death of a parent becomes real to an adult. Within the structure of the funeral ceremony are certain traditions including the saying of prayers, the singing of hymns, the reading of scriptures. These provide a consistent or stable background against which the actual mourning process can be enacted. There is the cohesiveness of friends and family coming together at a funeral, of being with other adults who may have shared similar experiences and whose sympathy is perceived, therefore, to be more genuine.

The stress caused by the death of a parent, while not always visible, can nevertheless be immense. Perhaps the most difficult aspect is becoming accustomed to the absence of someone who has always been present, whether physically or emotionally, and whether in love or anger. It is the disruption of this stability, or constancy, that necessitates great sensitivity on the part of those who are most supportive. Often, it is among friends, rather than family, where this need is met. Friends are usually of a similar age and may share similar interests. Thus, they can provide the support, advice and companionship no longer provided by the dead parent.

Families who have experienced death are often surprised by the intensity of their grief a week or two after the funeral. Once the funeral is over, and the friends and family members have dispersed, many adults find that they finally have time to acknowledge their feelings. Sometimes too, people who have prided themselves on their self-sufficiency find it difficult to accept support of any kind during this period. One of my patients simply refused any help when her mother died. The kind offers of relatives and friends were politely, but firmly, refused. In fact, they found themselves the recipients of her constant activity – cooking, baking, vacuuming, making cups of tea – and all because she could not allow her mind to rest and absorb the loss. Needless to say, she found her mother's death excruciatingly painful, and it was only after many weeks of encouragement and coaxing that she was able to begin to express the powerful emotions that she had been feeling.

The price we pay for being close to another person is the pain and grief we endure when we lose that person. As human beings, we respond to that loss, sooner or later, with a complex process of mourning. This process is absolutely essential and time-consuming, and any attempt to disrupt it carries the risk of emotional damage. Many adults are shocked and frightened by the emotions they experience after the death of a parent. Denial is often the initial reaction, and it may be several days before an adult can truly accept that a parent is gone forever. The adult, who only a matter of hours or days earlier was also the child in a family structure, has had that role destroyed forever.

If a parent's death occurs after a chronic and debilitating illness the denial of death may be less intense, but the grief is no less real. The denial is simply the mind's way of saying, "I cannot cope with so much pain at once." Once an adult is actually able to face a parent's death, he or she may begin to suffer from a host of strange and perhaps completely new physical symptoms: a tightening or lump in the throat; a tingling feeling of tension or edginess; heaviness in the limbs, extreme weakness and fatigue; loss of appetite and/or interest in sex are all part of the body's response to severe and prolonged stress.

Among the serious issues which require confrontation when a parent dies are feelings of anger, frustration and guilt. Often an adult will grow apart from a parent – perhaps living in a different city, perhaps holding opposing views on various issues or perhaps feeling jealousy towards a sibling whom the parent has favoured. Such diminishing contact, much of it inevitable, can result in an almost intractable guilt when the so-called "neglected" parent dies. Whether the guilt is real or imagined, it is too late to even consider the possibility of making amends. Unfortunately, as is often the case, those situations which cannot be resolved begin to assume an unreasonable importance, and professional counselling is often required.

The Will

Too often today, the family that endures the death of a parent will harbour astonishing feelings of jealousy, distrust and, in some cases, even hatred. In families where parents act as power brokers and quite literally play their children for love, where praise and affection are used as manipulative techniques and where sibling rivalry is unwittingly (but no less effectively) encouraged, the effects are devastating. Adults who are raised in such family settings will never have the opportunity to acquire the emotional maturity and the self-esteem necessary for stable adult relationships. Nowhere are these unresolved relationships more graphically displayed than when the contents of the dead parent's will are revealed. We all know of, or have read about, families that have been torn apart by the contents of such documents long after the author is dead and buried.

Pearl and the members of her family all suffered from feelings of low esteem, and the destructive forces within the family structure were revealed by her father's will:

> Nobody in my family ever got along very well. Even before my father died, it felt like we were always at each other's throats. My father had worked hard and had saved quite a bit of money – nobody knew exactly how much – and we all speculated about who would get what when he died. I think that my father got pleasure out of having kept this a secret. It meant that everyone treated him well, whether they wanted to or not, out of fear of losing out on what might be their share of the inheritance.

> When my dad finally died and we got together in the lawyer's office for the reading of the will, we were barely on speaking terms, we were all so tense.

> As it turned out, he had hundreds of thousands of dollars stashed away in term deposits. And do you know what he did with it? The son-of-a-bitch donated just about all of it to charity. The only relative who got anything was my daughter and the only reason she got it was because she married a man he'd always liked.

Maybe I should have seen it coming. I don't know that he was much of a father. He never really loved anything, I don't think, except making more money. But my brothers are absolutely furious and my daughter got what should have been mine. I was the one who looked after him when my mother died, not her. She never did a goddamned thing, except to marry someone he approved of.

Obviously, a will involves far more than the simple legal disposition of material goods. More significantly perhaps, it is the expression of real and perceived family relationships. It is the means by which a parent can control his children in death, just as surely as he did in life. Unfortunately, for those adults with the courage and confidence to defy this bizarre control from the grave, the penalty is often isolation from the family as a whole.

On the other hand, of course, a will can be the expression of sincere affection, fairness and integrity, particularly in a family where love and honesty have prevailed. Sometimes, when parents and children are aware of and are anxious to avoid creating a legacy of guilt and bitterness, reconciliation can be affected prior to death. Thus, the anger does not become a tradition to be passed from one generation to the next.

Another of my patients, Mrs. M., came to my office suffering from symptoms of anxiety and depression. Mrs. M.'s childhood had been neither easy nor happy. Her father, a most successful businessman, was a tyrant, and my patient's mother had sheltered her throughout her childhood from his anger and criticism. During her adolescence, Mrs. M. had rebelled against her authoritarian father and the household had become a battleground for their constant arguments.

At university, she met and married a man whom she perceived to be much kinder than her father, but soon discovered that, in addition to playing the same manipulative and controlling games her father had played, her husband was also an alcoholic.

During the course of her treatment, which began about

fifteen years after her marriage (and during which she found the courage to divorce her husband), Mrs. M.'s father became seriously ill. Summoning up the nerve to visit him, Mrs. M. found her father to be weak and his emotions more vulnerable than she could ever remember. He talked to her for the first time about his own background – about his family's poverty and about his own illegitimate birth – having hidden this knowledge from his wife and children, believing that it would serve no useful purpose for them to know.

Perhaps realizing the seriousness of his illness, and that the time for speaking openly was running short, he also expressed concern about Mrs. M. in her own marriage. To Mrs. M.'s surprise and sadness, he said that he regretted his treatment of her during her childhood and wished that he had contributed more to her self-esteem, even if they didn't always agree. He felt responsible, he said, for the fact that she had chosen a man who treated her so shabbily, because she was duplicating the precise environment in which she had been raised.

When her father had finished talking, Mrs. M. told him about how much she had wanted his love and his acceptance when she had been growing up. When she began crying, he reached out his hand to her and the two of them hugged each other. When she left, both father and daughter were exhausted, but each felt the beginnings of a reconciliation.

Mrs. M.'s father died shortly afterwards, but because both had done their best to reconcile their differences, Mrs. M. was able to mourn his death, knowing that she had, at least, begun to understand her father, and perhaps even to like him. He, in turn, had been sufficiently moved by her visit to rearrange his will and more equitably distribute his wealth. Needless to say, this provided Mrs. M. with a heightened sense of self-worth and a renewed determination to carry on this newly-found legacy of honesty and integrity. Since that time, Mrs. M. has remarried and now shares a much happier life with a man who embodies many of her father's better qualities.

Not every family, of course, will be able to achieve Mrs. M.'s happy ending. In fact, it is sometimes impossible to resolve unhappy relationships, particularly if they have become a way of life. Still, an attempt to reconcile differences before an older parent dies may prevent the will from becoming an instrument of further destruction and bitterness.

The best hope for any family is that the good things within the family structure – integrity, honesty, feelings of respect, a sense of responsibility and a commitment to excellence – can be passed from generation to generation. The tremendous burden of such a legacy is often sustained by one member of a family who acts as a responsible benefactor; willing and able to share his inherent strength and goodness with the others in the family, providing the link between generations.

In coping with the death of a parent, it is most important for the survivor to know that he has done his best with his or her parent in life, and to know that being honest and open with one another can eliminate the inevitable anguish when there is no time left to talk it over. For those who have fully developed their own lives, who have pursued individual interests and activities, but who have never lost sight of the significance of the relationship between parents and children, grieving can be a normal and strengthening part of life.

VII
WIDOW

In North American society the chances are very high that a wife will eventually become a widow. In fact, there are about four times as many widows as there are widowers, partly because women have a longer life expectancy than men, and also because husbands are often older than their wives and thus are likely to die sooner.

A widow whose husband has recently died is probably going through one of the most stressful periods of her life. The married years of sharing dreams and disappointments, hopes and frustrations are over, as she becomes part of a large segment of society: women who lose and mourn their husbands and then slowly begin to rebuild their lives.

Heart disease is the leading cause of death both in Canada and the United States. Heart attacks strike more men than women and often those who have no prior awareness of heart disease. It is often this kind of death, so sudden and so unexpected, which proves to be the most difficult with which to cope. Surprisingly enough, about twenty percent of all widows in North America are under forty-five years of age and it is these women, whose husbands die unexpectedly, who have the most difficult financial, emotional and social adjustments of all.

Cancer is the second most common killer and is usually associated with lingering illness prior to the actual death. A wife often finds herself wishing, for everyone's sake, that her husband would die quickly. This is not a genuine desire to hasten the death, but simply an attempt to halt the suffering.

However such feelings can produce a tremendous amount of guilt when the death finally occurs.

It is significant to realize that there is no intentional disloyalty in such thoughts, nor should there be any regret for not having done more. In addition, despite the opportunity a cancer patient's wife may have to prepare for his death, there may be a reaction of total disbelief when it actually occurs. For many months a wife may have been visiting the hospital or acting as a nurse at home, so that when the death actually occurs, the shock of no longer being someone's wife, but suddenly a widow, is overwhelming. A widow is faced not only with grieving for her dead husband, but also with finding and consolidating for herself a new role in society as a single woman.

In the first days following her husband's death, the widow is still recoiling from the shock which often varies with the degree to which she was prepared. At this stage, acceptance is still confused with denial of the death. A woman may find herself crying over her husband's death, yet in the next moment find herself setting a place for him at dinner. Part of her accepts the knowledge while part of her continues to reject it.

Grief and the stress of grieving affect people in a variety of ways. Many cannot imagine that they will ever feel better, although eventually they do. The process of grieving cannot be hurried. It is hard and painfully exhausting work, but essential for the restructuring of one's own life. Some widows are unable to eat or sleep, some become dizzy and develop headaches, still others suffer from chest pains or heart palpitations. Many women become ill themselves after their husbands die, often developing frighteningly similar symptoms. The most universal problem is depression, but it is an integral part of the work of mourning and must be experienced before it can be overcome.

One woman, Mrs. H, described her experiences in the following way:

My husband died at our yacht club seven years ago of a

heart attack. I was forty seven at the time. I was at home that day with my three teenagers and my three-year-old daughter when I heard a knock at the door. When I opened the door I was surprised to see two of our friends from the yacht club. They said, "John has had some sort of an attack, and we've come to take you to the hospital." I said to myself, "He's dead." I just knew it.

I was very calm before I left the house, and I didn't say a word to anyone about my feeling. My only reaction was a dryness. I could hardly talk I was so dry. On the way to the hospital we drove by the lake, and I thought about my husband's love for the water. He had owned a boat for fifteen years, and spent many, many hours in his boat on that lake. John loved sailing so much that at times I was jealous of the boat and the water. As we were driving by it was a beautiful sunny day, the water was sparkling and I said to myself, "Lake, you won."

When we got to the hospital I was rushed into a little room by one of the doctors and he said, "Mrs. H., did you know your husband was dead on arrival." I remained calm when I heard those terrible words, but the dryness I felt in my body overwhelmed me. I didn't cry – as a matter of fact I don't cry at death very often. I cry when I hear beautiful music or see a parade. I guess I was just so stunned, that I could not comprehend that John was really dead.

After the death there were things I had to do which I never thought of before. Like going to the cemetery to choose a plot. I never knew you had to pay on the spot. We had a few hundred dollars in our joint chequing account, but our savings account and safety deposit box were in John's name. When he died they were both sealed, and I couldn't get at them until some time later. By the time the funeral came, I ran out of money. Thank goodness my family were there to help me. I don't know what I would have done without all their support.

Although I don't remember it in great detail, I think the whole process of the funeral was a good thing. I met friends there and immediately got over that difficult task of seeing them. There were a few friends who could not

come to the funeral, and I dreaded seeing them after-
wards. Later on when I saw them for the first time as
John's widow it brought back painful memories of being
with them as John's wife.

When the funeral was over Mrs. H. began to develop physical symptoms which concerned her. Many women who are
grieving for the loss of a loved one experience physical as well
as psychological disturbances. Mrs. H. described her symptoms:

> A funny thing happened to me in those next few days. I
> had a feeling that there was a wall around me which was
> about two feet thick. It was as if nobody could get to me
> because of this wall. It was a very peculiar feeling, and I
> suddenly felt completely alone. The other really intense
> feeling I had was that of a broken heart – literally. There
> was a heavy feeling, as if there were weights on my heart.
> The wall around me and the heaviness in my chest lasted
> for about a year.

> I was very busy for a while. I had to find so many pieces of
> paper like my marriage certificate, see lawyers and ac-
> countants and settle John's business partnership. About a
> week after the funeral, when things had settled down a bit,
> a friend came to visit me. Suddenly I felt all my strength
> leaving me and I said to her, "I'm going to pass out." I
> began to shake, my heart began to beat very rapidly and I
> started to cry uncontrollably.

> She called my doctor who is also my next door neighbour.
> When he took one look at me he said, "This is what I have
> been waiting for." It was a delayed reaction. Suddenly I
> realized that my husband was dead and buried, and that he
> was never coming back again. Everybody had to go
> through this intense grief sooner or later. I was terribly
> shaky for months afterwards, and would sometimes cry for
> no apparent reason.

> I visited the cemetery after John's death, but more be-
> cause I felt it was expected of me than for any other rea-
> son. I'm a Catholic and, because of my deep religious be-
> lief, I feel his soul has gone to heaven and what is left in

the grave is really just a shell. Some widows find great peace by going to their husbands' graves and just sitting there, but it doesn't do anything for me. One of my daughters goes quite regularly, but the other children don't. My religion taught me that death was part of life. When my husband died, I felt it was God's prerogative to take him from me. We all have to face it sometime. Despite that I still suffered a great personal loss when he died and felt very alone for a long time.

Mrs. H. expressed her feelings about having her children with her:

Thank goodness for my four kids. They are what kept me going. It must be just awful to come home to an empty house. If the kids weren't there, I'm sure I wouldn't cook for myself, I'd just grab any old thing. Children are a great blessing at times like that, as long as they're good kids. Having problems with them when you are grieving would be too much to bear.

It's amazing how the children seemed to bounce back, and a week later they wanted to go to a school dance. I tried playing on my son's sympathy, telling him I was terribly lonely and asking him to stay home with me. His answer was that he couldn't really help me with my loneliness. He was right. He wouldn't have done me one bit of good by sitting home with me. Kids have to carry on with their own lives, but I don't think one realizes how hurt they really are inside.

I feel sorry for my youngest. She was only three when her father died. I had her when I was forty-four and she is much younger than her brother and sisters. I feel sorry for her when the other children at school talk about what their fathers do. When Father's Day comes, and they make cards for their fathers, she makes one out to her uncle. She often says to me, "Please get married again because I want a Daddy." I tease her and say, "We'll put an ad in the paper saying, 'Wanted: rich man, kind and gentle, to be a husband and father.' "

My children are the most important people in my life now. Losing a husband is a terrible thing for any woman to go through, but I can't imagine losing a child. I think that would be the most horrible thing that could happen. You think about their whole lives ahead of them. I'm sure if my kids were taken away from me, I would just be done in. I couldn't bear it – no doubt about it.

The funeral is an extremely important event in which the bereaved family must participate. Any widow who cannot believe that her husband is actually dead will be left with no doubts after the funeral and burial rituals are over. Often well-meaning friends and even doctors may encourage the use of tranquilizers and sedatives before and during the funeral. It is not a good idea to be sedated however. Rather, it is important to have a clear memory of the funeral for that is the point at which the survivors actually begin to say goodbye. A widow will recount the funeral scene innumerable times in the days which follow and painful as it may be, it does help her to begin to accept her loss.

Similarly, many women feel obliged to remain calm and emotionless during the ceremony. North American society tends to view with great admiration the woman who doesn't cry at her husband's funeral. "Wasn't she marvellous and brave?" To deny the pain and sadness is to deny the loss and to reject the support of family and friends who are present.

After the funeral ritual a widow may, for the first time in her life, be coming home alone to an empty house. A woman who lost her husband after her children had all grown up and left home is typical of the widows who have to come home to empty houses for the first time in their lives. In those first weeks of bereavement all she could think about was her husband. In the subsequent months she found some times more painful than others. Anniversaries, birthdays, the day he first heard his diagnosis and the first anniversary of his death were all difficult times she had to face alone.

Like many other women in her situation, after a couple of years she decided it was time to stop feeling sorry for herself. She started doing some part-time work at a local hospital and also enrolled in one university course. She said to me:

I felt as if part of me died when my husband died. For a long time all I did was mope around the house and watch television. One day I woke up and it struck me that I was sixty years old and with any luck I could still live another fifteen years. I started thinking about death and realized that I would be dead for a long time, so why not enjoy life while I could. That day my life changed and I knew that people can't grieve forever. I loved my husband and I think of him often, but I also have a responsibility to myself.

Like so many major transitions in life such as marriage and childbirth, for which many people are ill-prepared, widowhood brings a number of very practical problems as well. It is a stage in life which so many women will face but is accorded virtually no thought or preparation until it occurs. Once the period of intense grieving has passed (and this may take as long as two years) a widow must face a redefinition of her status in a society which, unfortunately, tends to regard women in terms of their marital status.

Many women do emerge from their grieving with plans for creating a new life; many more, however, are so troubled that they never do recover from their husband's death and they exist for the rest of their lives in deep despair. A woman whose husband handled all aspects of their life outside the home may find herself completely lost when he dies. Some women are totally ignorant of their husband's earnings, insurance coverage or investments. A few have not even been allowed to write cheques.

Such women, when they become widows, may find themselves dealing with lawyers, insurance agents and garage mechanics for the first time in their lives. They must cope not only with their grief for their husbands, but also with the added burden of an unfamiliar set of circumstances. In addition the care of young children (if any) will now fall solely on the widow, particularly if her husband had shared in the child care routine. Although at first a widow can often feel lost as a single parent, the presence of children can prove very therapeutic.

Although Mrs. H. was in the fortunate position of being able to stay at home to care for her children, many widows are not. It is often both stressful and embarrassing to go job-hunting with little or no recent experience and widows are often forced, in desperation, to take low-paying and sometimes demeaning jobs. Sometimes widows who are left short of money but who have small children to support must depend on welfare or on the generosity of relatives. This can be an uncomfortable situation at best and can gnaw away at whatever self-respect such widows can muster.

One young widow had not been away from her four year old twins for more than a few hours in three years. She couldn't afford a babysitter nor had she had a holiday in all that time. Finally she decided to move back to her parents' home for financial reasons, but it was very hard on her because she was treated like a child again. She had to tell her parents where and with whom she was going, and when she would be back, just as she did in her adolescence. She got away from the children more often, but had to pay a price for it.

There is a danger, of course, that a widow with no children to care for and no job requiring attention will be overwhelmed by her grief and will centre her whole existence on her sadness. It is essential for a married woman to consider the possibility of facing the future as a widow and to make every attempt to establish herself as a person with her own identity before it actually happens.

Perhaps the loneliness is the most difficult aspect of widowhood, particularly the loss of companionship and of a sexual relationship. Some women immediately plunge into a series of casual affairs, while others find themselves fending off the advances of friends' husbands. Often a widow finds herself loathing her single life and wanting to remarry as soon as possible.

A fifty year old widow described how she felt in social situation:

As a single woman again, you have to avoid feeling hurt all

the time. You are not treated like a married woman, and even a woman who has never married. You feel like an extra person, because you are always alone. If you are at a dance and are sitting with a couple the husband won't dance with his wife because he doesn't feel it is right to leave you alone at the table. I often refuse invitations because I just don't want to go alone. When I do go out alone, I feel so lonely when I see couples all around me. It's very hard to fight the loneliness.

The actual rate of remarriage among the widowed is considerably lower for women than for men, partly because there are so many more widows than widowers and perhaps because some women during their married years have become fairly passive about forming new relationships.

Mrs. H. feels that, for her, loneliness is one of the worst aspects of widowhood:

It's hard not to feel lonely when all your friends are enjoying life with their husbands. I think, on the whole, your friends are marvellous to you for the first few months, but after that they are inclined to forget about you. A lot of widows find they are slowly dropped because we are living in a couple-oriented society.

Unless you know the people, you feel like a fifth wheel. You are more inclined to see the women alone for lunch rather than going out with a couple. The other thing I learned very early was to take myself wherever I was going rather than relying on rides. This enables me to leave if I'm not enjoying myself without having to wait for the people who brought me.

I think you can get to feel sorry for yourself if you allow it. The other day when I was listening to the radio, they played a lovely piece of music. I thought, wouldn't it be nice to be with a man who held me close and just danced around with me in his arms. Then I had a terrible washed out feeling of just desperate loneliness. It doesn't happen to me that often because I keep very busy but it does happen occasionally.

The worst times for me are the week-ends – they are just

hell. Week-ends are a time when couples are together. I wouldn't think of phoning a friend to go to lunch on a Saturday. The summers are also very lonely because friends go away.

It's very difficult being a single woman after twenty years of marriage. Where in heavens name do you go to meet men? There are single parent organizations, but a lot of divorced people go there. Widows are really quite different from divorced people, and a widow likes to be known as a widow.

I know a man who lost his wife six months ago. He had made some overtures towards me recently at the yacht club but I walked away, because I thought it was too soon after his wife died for him to be flirting with women.

I thought it over in the next few days, and decided to invite him to my home for a drink. This was the first man I had been interested in since my husband's death seven years earlier. It took all my courage to telephone him and invite him over. I deliberated for three days, and finally I called him. The night he came I thought he'd never leave – it was one o'clock in the morning before he went home. I have seen him a couple of times since then, but nothing much has developed.

Although remarriage must be a very personal kind of decision, it can be a very positive step for widows who have integrated their first husband's death and put it in its proper perspective. It is also important to avoid being unduly influenced by one's children who may or may not want a new father. Mrs. H. occasionally thinks about remarriage:

Seven years have passed now. I have grown used to a new way of life and have learned to be very independent. My three oldest children have all left home, and my youngest is at school all day. I am involved in a Widow's Aid group, as well as some church work which keeps me very busy. I'm really ambivalent about marrying again. Sometimes I don't think I would want to get up on a regular basis and cook a man's breakfast, wash his socks, and have to put up with his likes and dislikes.

But then again, I guess I haven't fallen in love. If we are all honest with ourselves we have to admit we are looking for somebody. You have to think about whether you want to spend the rest of your life alone, or get the love and companionship that might come out of a new relationship. Sometimes I wonder what would happen if that person became sick. Could I face nursing someone through a lingering illness? Maybe I'm a very selfish person, but I'm afraid maybe the next one will die on me too.

I don't think about my own death very often, and when I do it is in relation to my youngest daughter. Life has been a little unfair to her. I feel like her grandmother now because I'm so much older than her friends' mothers and she has had to grow up without a father. All I pray is that I will live long enough to allow me to take care of my little one until she grows up and can take care of herself.

In any discussion of the general kinds of problems facing new widows it is useful to mention some of the unusually distorted or delayed grief reactions which may unnecessarily frighten some widows. Often excessive activity represents an unusual response to grief. Such activities can include promiscuity, constant travelling, continually buying clothes, or perpetually redecorating a house. Some women do not experience grief immediately following but have delayed reactions much later.

One woman appeared to be having a heart attack when she was recovering from some major surgery. Medically there was no proof that it was her heart but she continued to experience severe chest pains. After a great deal of probing it turned out that her husband had died on that day, 15 years earlier. The circumstances of his death were quite unusual. He had been in the Air Force during the war and had been reported missing and presumed dead. She had no further news about him for three years and in her mind she had buried him, and had made all the adjustments for a new life.

One day she received word that her husband was alive after all, and was coming home. Although she was happy he was alive, she no longer wanted to resume the marriage because she had met a new man whom she wanted to marry. She was planning to ask her husband for a divorce when he came home. The day he was due to arrive home she went to meet him at the airport. When he stepped off the plane and before she had a chance to talk to him he suddenly dropped dead of a heart attack. However, she never grieved for him and went on with her life as usual. Suddenly, fifteen years later, this woman had a delayed grief reaction which overwhelmed her at a time when she was very vulnerable, and she spent the next few weeks crying and mourning before she could carry on again.

The reason for this widow's delayed grief reaction is rather complex. She and her husband were having marital problems before he went to war. Thus, she had sometimes secretly wished he would get killed because it would solve her problems. When he was reported missing, however, she felt very guilty about having wished him harm.

After three years when she received word he was returning she was happy he was alive because it relieved her guilt. On the other hand it created new problems for her because she didn't want to resume the marriage. When he died she felt relieved because it meant she didn't have to deal with the conflict, but once again she felt guilty for feeling relieved. She was unable to grieve for him because doing so would have meant facing up to all her deepest emotions. Fifteen years later, at a time when she was very vulnerable, she had a grief reaction.

Despite the fact that it may seem unnecessarily morbid, it is essential that couples plan for the death of one or the other by making reasonable financial plans and by arranging for adequate insurance coverage. Business arrangements, including investment holdings, should also be familiar to both members of the marriage partnership and both husbands and wives should draw up wills. A wife should also ensure that she has joint account privileges as any funds, in an account held only by her husband, will be frozen on his death. Access to a bank account or other personal funds will ensure that the widow can pay for the funeral and have enough money to live on until the will is probated.

It is essential too that a wife be completely (and quickly) open with her children when her husband dies. It is as sad for children to lose a father as it is for a wife to lose a husband. They must know exactly what has happened, seeing their mother's sadness will help to acknowledge their own.

Many women make the mistake of treating their dead husband as if he were still alive. Giving his clothes away and admitting that he is gone is only the beginning, but it is a significant step. A widow living alone in a house might want to consider moving into a smaller home or an apartment where the upkeep and repairs are handled by someone else. This is a decision which requires careful consideration, however. No one should be forced to move unwillingly or impulsively. There is often concern over poor nutrition in persons living alone. This concern is, of course, magnified when a widow is depressed as well as alone. A widow who is anxious about being alone might want to consider a pet. A cat, or a dog can provide companionship and security.

When a widow finds herself sufficiently self-assured to seek out people again she may find herself in the position of having to do the actual "seeking." A widow may have to reach out to people herself, asking about friends who might want companionship, accepting social invitations in the hopes of meeting new people, attending single parent functions or going to lectures or plays.

A widow must realize, as well, that she is not betraying her dead husband by enjoying the friendship of another man. The longer a woman is married to her husband, the greater the readaptation in lifestyle when he dies. However, no one person can ever replace another. That is impossible because we are all unique and thus all relationships are unique. A widow, of any age and in any circumstances, must learn to adapt to and to value new people, new activities, and new relationships, as well as to cherish the memory of what has gone before.

VIII
WIDOWER

Although traditional roles in North American society are changing the majority of husbands still work to support their families, and their wives (although they often contribute to the total income) tend to be responsible for running the household and the care of children. Most husbands help their wives with some household duties and occasional babysitting, but few actually share equally in the domestic tasks. It is generally the wife who cooks, cleans, does laundry, organizes entertainment and cares for the children.

Furthermore, in most families it is the father who reflects the "outside world" in the home. Through their husbands and fathers, wives and children not only view the working world, but also formulate their own image of what a grown man should be like. Because of this traditional structuring of society, many men have simply never learned to run a household or to care for children. This can have devastating implications, in a very practical sense, for a man who is widowed.

In the part of the marriage not involving children or household responsibilities, husbands and wives share a more equal kind of dependency. Husbands and wives rely on one another for emotional sustenance, for comfort, for support and for companionship. Husbands and wives rely heavily on each other's skills as well. A shy husband may rely on his wife's social skills, or a wife may feel uncomfortable doing repairs around the house and may prefer to have her husband do them. Problems arise when the reliance becomes maladaptive, when one person feels totally empty and worthless without the other. Sadly, this can happen when a husband becomes a widower.

As in the case of a widow, a widower finds his way of life drastically altered when his wife dies. He must not only adjust to the loneliness of living without a partner, but also begin to act as both mother and father to his children. Most widowers are not faced with the same financial worries which confront many widows. But they do have to endure the same loss of a friend and a lover, a partner in conversations, in disputes, in love and in the pattern of everyday life. Everything which a wife has contributed to her husband's life, all the memories she has shared and all the amusing stories which made her laugh are suddenly all part of the past.

In our society some men do not show any visible sign of emotion. Crying is viewed as an indication of weakness, of vulnerability. As a result these men find it difficult to express their grief openly. They tend to adopt a "business as usual" kind of attitude and thus thwart the essential grieving process.

One lawyer, who got a call that his wife had finally died after a lingering illness, finished his day at court as usual after he heard the news. This man wanted no scenes and no tears, but he was really denying his pain and grief. He held a private memorial service very quickly and cremated his wife's body, so that the entire matter was over and done with in a couple of days.

As a result he never came to terms with the fact that his wife had died, and after a few months turned to alcohol to counteract his depression.

This man was typical of those who block out what they are really feeling. Often they will begin to become extremely angry about the loss, thinking, "How could she do this to me. How could she leave me when I am in my prime and things are going so well?" Because the anger generates guilt which he cannot allow to surface, he denies the whole event. The grieving process is essential however, and any attempt to ignore or deny it will eventually take its toll. It is essential for a husband to be honest with himself, to acknowledge his anger, frustration and sorrow over his wife's death, as these feelings are all integral parts of losing a loved one and will eventually mellow.

Many men feel "broken hearted" after their wife's death and this is not a term to be scoffed at. The whole notion of a "broken heart" has persisted for many hundreds of years, and in earlier times, "grief" was commonly listed as a cause of death. Certainly it is a statistical fact that widowers have a higher mortality rate during the first year of bereavement than do married men of the same age, and the most common cause of death in the group is heart disease. While it has not been proven that grief causes heart disease, links exist between increased stress, excessive drinking and smoking, and changes in diet following a spouse's death.

Mr. R., a forty-seven-year-old civil servant, had been married to his wife for twenty-five years. They had three daughters, aged seventeen, nineteen and twenty-one and led a quiet but happy life. He tells what happened to his family in this way:

> With the girls grown up we were just starting to enjoy our freedom, and life seemed very good. Although I don't have a lot of money, we had just bought two rooms of new furniture, and were planning our first big holiday without the family. My sister and brother-in-law were visiting us from Ireland when it happened. One day we were all out at a restaurant when suddenly my wife collapsed. She was in a lot of pain and the sweat was just pouring off her. She could still talk and said she thought it was her heart. The ambulance arrived pretty quickly and I had the choice of riding with her or following in my car. Since my relatives were with me, I decided to follow the ambulance. The ambulance took about ten minutes to get to the hospital and by the time she arrived she was dead. She was only forty-five years old.
>
> I was in a state of shock when they told me she was dead. I couldn't believe it. All I could think of was that those guys

in the ambulance didn't do anything to help her. I kept going over it in my mind and wondering if things would have been any different had I been in the ambulance with her. I kept wondering if they tried to resuscitate her in any way, or if they even looked at her – they certainly should have. If only I had been with her . . .

Around the time of the funeral I was thankful to have my relatives with me. My sister, coming from Belfast, is used to bombs going off all the time. All the ladies in that city live on Valium pills, and she had hundreds of them with her. I took some and so did my girls. They helped us survive the funeral. My youngest daughter must have taken a few because after the funeral she told me she felt like she wasn't really there. She felt like she was watching it from far away. I guess you have to take something to help you through it. Even a glass of whisky would help the pain.

At the time I was so lost, and it was very hard for me to make any decisions. I remember thinking I wish we had made arrangements for burial long ago in the event of either of our deaths. That way you don't have to make any decisions when you are in such a bad way. Another thing you don't realize is that you have to pay the cemetery on the spot, and you'd better have the money. When you are in such a state of shock after a death you don't think about practical things.

Now I realize that you can save money by planning ahead because the cemeteries in the city cost much more than those on the outskirts. I've been telling some of the guys at work to make plans now, before anyone gets sick, but they would rather not think about it. I guess I used to be the same way. If you don't plan for it you think it can't happen. But it does.

It really hit me hard after the funeral was over. A week and a half after my wife died I started getting chest pains. I ignored them because they weren't too bad, but three days later I was admitted to hospital with a heart attack two weeks after my wife died of the same thing. At that point I didn't really care if I lived or died. I didn't have much to live for.

Mr. R. had been very dependent on his wife to take care of him and their daughters and did not have many of his own friends. When his wife died he was at a loss because his whole life had revolved around her. After he had his heart attack he was at the lowest point in his life, both physically and emotionally:

> I guess my daughters must have been pretty worried. I stayed in the hospital for a month, and then I came back home. I don't know what I would have done without my girls. They took care of me. They did everything around the house, all the cooking and the cleaning. They even arranged for the Salvation Army to get all my wife's clothes. I guess the girls took the whole thing pretty hard, but we don't discuss it very often. Maybe we should – I don't know. Every time I try to talk about it my eyes fill with tears, and I can barely talk. I don't talk much, but I think about it all the time. Her death is on my mind all day long. Sometimes I think I hear footsteps and I think she's back, but then it passes.

> My girls seem to be coping better than I am, at least it would appear that way. I think they behave better now than they ever did. I've had no trouble with them, but also I've been careful not to cause any trouble too, because they could just leave if they wanted to, and I would be all alone.

> I've known kids who have left home just over words they had with their parents, so I let the girls do pretty much what they want. They don't do anything bad. They don't smoke marijuana or drink alcohol. I guess I'm lucky I wasn't left with a couple of wild boys. My girls grew up in a hurry when their mother died, and they are all I have now. I guess some day they will leave me and make their own lives. I don't know what I'll do then.

Mr. R. did the same thing with his daughters that he had done with his wife. He put them in a position of having to take care of him. Instead of taking the initiative and helping them with their problems, he has reverted to a passive role. It is unfortunate for the whole family that he has not been able to discuss his depression with his daughters, because he has no outlet for his intense feelings. He was afraid to talk to his daughters because he feared he would break down in front of them and that would be too embarrassing for him. If Mr. R. had communicated with his daughters it would have helped everyone involved and deepened the family bonds:

> Being back at work again is a great comfort to me, because it keeps me busy. I would go crazy if I couldn't work, because my work keeps my mind off the past. It's funny, I used to work on a rescue squad and saw so many deaths in my day: hangings, murders, suicides, and drownings. They never affected me that much. When it's someone you love it's so different.

> Sometimes I think about heart disease and it just doesn't make sense to me. I've seen drunks and derelicts who have had heart attacks and survived, and then there's a woman like my wife – only forty-five. She was really cheated. I think about my own heart disease too. They tell me I may have to have heart surgery, but I don't worry about it too much. If my heart lasts another five years I will be happy. It's funny, last year when I was forty-six I thought I was still young. This year I feel very old.

> The hardest part for me is being alone. We didn't have a wide circle of friends, and we always did things together. I get very lonely at night when I'm in bed. That's when I miss her most. I want to reach out and hold her in my arms again and then I feel so alone. People tell me that I can remarry, that I'm still young, but I wouldn't consider remarriage, not in my condition. My heart could give out at any time and it wouldn't be fair.

> My wife's death and my own illness have made me think a lot about life and death. I really loved my wife, and I guess now I'm paying the price for losing someone you love. The only way you could avoid this pain is by not getting too attached. But how can someone not get too attached. Life just wouldn't be worthwhile.

At this point it was still only three months after Mr. R.'s wife's death and he was still deeply distraught. Unless Mr. R. regains some of his will to live, and begins to take care of himself and his family, he will live a lonely life, acting and appearing far older than his years.

In sharp contrast, is Mr. S., a successful businessman. He too, was widowed, but had a remarkably different set of problems to face:

> About a month before I married her, my wife told me she had been a diabetic since she was 18, She had never mentioned it before, and assured me that it was a private disease and that she would look after it by herself. She told me she would not live to be hundred, but that she could have a fairly normal life for many years.
>
> In my experience I have found diabetics to be a peculiar group of people and I would even venture to say they have very different personalities from other people. They are usually very beautiful people, lovely people, but they have many complexes and problems. Diabetics are given a set of rules by which they must live their lives, the most important being their diet and medication, but many of them cheat.
>
> My wife cheated all the time, but she was only cheating herself. She went to the doctor once a month, and a week before she went she starved herself to get her blood sugar into shape. I told her she wasn't taking good care of herself. I talked and talked, but it was like talking to the wall. There's a mental attitude involved in diabetics, and if you have a lousy attitude, what chance have you got?

Mr. S.'s wife died a very tragic death when she was only forty-six. All her life she had been an attractive, smartly dressed woman. She was very sophisticated and always projected a certain image to the outside world. The first thing that happened to her when she started going down hill was that she sprained her ankle which did not heal properly. As a result, her feet became swollen, and she couldn't wear the right shoes to go with her outfits. Once she could not be properly co-ordinated, her whole self-image began to deteriorate. Next, she developed clots in her eyes and started to lose her eyesight. With her failing eyesight she could not apply makeup properly, and again the image she had of herself faltered:

It was very sad when she began losing her eyesight. She was afraid of the dark, and was terrified of going blind which would mean total darkness for the rest of her life. She eventually did go blind, before her death, but by then she had given up her fight. It was one problem after another for poor Terry. She was very susceptible to infections and developed several bladder and kidney infections. Often her severe diabetes went completely out of control. She and I had some dramatic times. Sometimes she would wake up in the middle of the night and say over and over, "I wish I were dead."

I knew that Terry was going to give up on life if she couldn't live the type of life she was used to. When she was sad, I cried with her but somehow I could never reach her during that time. During our twenty-five years of marriage we had never developed a method of communicating that was really good.

I was out in the business world and I was learning and changing all the time. She didn't keep up with what was happening in the outside world. As long as she had her children and her society she was content. We were quite happy together. We had a good family life, and many social relationships which kept us very busy. I guess we were always too busy to really get to know one another and to communicate our deepest emotions.

I now look around and see that most of the people of our generation have the same type of marriages where there isn't much emphasis placed on understanding and reaching out to the partner on an emotional level. You have your role as a husband and father, and that is easy to follow. What is more difficult is going beyond that and exposing your soul to your partner. Terry didn't know the hell I was going through when she was sick. She couldn't reach me, and I guess I couldn't really reach her either.

Mr. and Mrs. S. are typical of the married couples who have been too busy all their lives to really get to know one another. Mr. S. was active in business and had all his stimulation outside the home. His home was his refuge where he came for peace and quiet, food and sex. He never spent time with his wife talking about what bothered her or what she needed. Mrs. S. kept busy by having a family as soon as they got married so that she did not have to be alone and her time was spent raising the children, visiting her friends and participating in all her social activities.

She turned a blind eye when her husband failed to come home some nights because their marriage was not one where problems were confronted and worked out. The two main things she wanted from her husband were security and financial support, both of which she received. They did love each other, but had never developed a deep level of communication and understanding. They both adhered to their respective roles and did not go beyond that:

> My wife didn't understand my inner turmoil. Because she was dying she was only concerned with herself. I tried to be a dutiful husband, staying with her as much as I could and keeping up our sex life as long as possible. Finally I felt I had a choice to make – either I would stay with her every minute being a dutiful husband, or I would start to pull out to protect myself.

> It's a terrible choice to have to make with someone you love. For me she died a thousand deaths. She died a little more every time she sat up at night crying, "I wish I were dead." I cried with her, but eventually I couldn't take it any more and I started to draw away. One of my excuses to try to get some time for myself was that I said I had to work.

> Fortunately, my financial situation is such that I don't have to work and I could afford to take the time off, but I told Terry that I had to work sometime. Her reply was, "Sell everything, the business, the house, and stay here with me." I guess if I felt it could have saved her, or if I felt there was a future, I would have done it. I knew deep down it was all over.

> I went through a terrible time before her death. On the one hand I wanted to have some life for myself too. I felt very guilty about wanting something for myself, but what price does a living person have to pay when someone else

is dying? What my wife wanted from me was comforting and I guess I didn't know how to give it to her. I've learned since, but it's too late now.

The outside world considered me a saint because I was doing everything possible for her. I took her to a famous centre in another city where they specialize in the management of diabetes. For the first time they were able to regulate her blood pressure and diabetes, by controlling her diet and blood sugar. For her it was like being in jail. She was away from her home and her family, and she finally got fed up and came back home. When she got here, she caught pneumonia and almost died. She agreed to go back to the centre where she stayed for a while longer. Finally she came back home again, saying she was through with that and was back for good. She began to deteriorate pretty quickly, and two months later she just gave up. She said, "I'm going to die now," and four days later she died. She named her own day.

We had three children who ranged in age from nineteen to twenty- four, and they too ran away from my wife towards the end. They couldn't stand it anymore. My wife was not happy about anything. She was not accommodating, and was miserable a lot of the time. She was unable to cope with the children and they found her a burden. To come to their defence I think they tried their best to be with her, but they couldn't. I probably set the example.

The summer Terry died all the kids were away, everybody left her. We didn't expect her to die so rapidly. The doctors told her she would live at least another six months, so I told the kids they could go off on their summer vacations. She died when they were all away.

When she died I went into a state of shock and acted as if I were drunk or on some kind of drug. I was saying things that were very strange and completely out of character. When I look back I realized that I felt relief that she and I and the people around us didn't have to suffer anymore. It was over, and I felt like I was out of jail. I had many conflicting feelings that were all mixed together when she died, including guilt, relief and sadness. I didn't really face my loss right away. I'm getting over my pain and sadness at losing her now – almost two years later.

What I did to avoid grieving was throw myself into play. I met a lady and got involved with her right away. I transferred all the love and affection I felt for my wife to this lady. It was a lousy choice. We kept on the sham for a while, but pretty soon I realized my mistake. I didn't stop and figure out what my wife's death meant to me, and didn't give myself time to heal the wounds. When your partner dies, your psyche is not in good shape, and you are in no position to form a new relationship with anybody for a while. I would lay my life on it – if any man marries again within six months of losing his wife he is acting purely on the rebound. It's the easiest way of getting out of grieving, but only temporarily.

The kids have been affected by their mother's death in different ways. My youngest daughter had been running the household since she was fourteen. We had hired help, but she was really in charge while her mother was away. It has been devastating for her these last five years. My oldest daughter was married, but she got a divorce around the time her mother died. It was a terrible time for her too.

My son also suffered without a mother or father around to help him with his problems. I think the children have matured a great deal from the experience. They are far more grown up than the average person of their age because they were on their own so much. Death is a very sobering experience, but I think in our family's case it brought us closer together.

It took me a few months though, because immediately after Terry's death I wanted to run away from the whole situation. I said to my kids, "Look, I want a sabbatical. I've been a father for so many years, and I want a rest. Just pretend you don't have a father for a while." They were very hurt, and I now realize it was a rotten thing to say. I didn't realize at the time that I didn't want a sabbatical from my kids, I wanted one from myself – from my head.

I have since asked my kids for their forgiveness because I realized they were the most important people in my life.

We have grown really close. We talk about everything, and now have a good family life. They are grown up and I let them make their own decisions, but there is a great mutual respect.

Although I enjoy my family, I find that I have no routine to my life. One of the terrible things about losing a partner is that your whole life and all your routines are disrupted. I consider this period a hiatus. I feel as if there is no real direction to my life. When my wife died all my routines died with her. Things are very different for me now. I'm functioning well, but I miss the stability of having a loving wife at home.

Any relationship I may have now with a woman is not whole, it's fragmented. Being married for so many years gets you used to living with someone, and seeing her at proper hours, and having a decent type of existence, and I miss that. If I fall in love again, I would want to get married again.

Mr. S. is now at the stage where he has put his wife's death in its proper perspective and has begun to think about his own future realistically. He recognizes that he misses certain things which his wife provided, but that it would be foolish to rush into a marriage without love. The death was a sobering experience for him and he used it for real personal growth. He is more of a family man than he ever was before and now recognizes the value of a good family life.

In the days and weeks following his wife's death, a widower will experience a variety of feelings, many of them strange and bewildering. They may include fatigue, numbness, confusion, and a despondence so overwhelming that life may seem meaningless. Many widowers search for their wives, thinking they can see or hear them and they may feel as if they are going mad. While such experiences can be terrifying in their intensity, they are all part of the normal mourning process. They will pass slowly and the strength to carry on will gradually be regained.

After the funeral ritual is over, the widower will come

home to a changed household. Tasks must be re-allocated and children cared for. A housekeeper can deal with the cooking and cleaning, but she is not a mother and it will be the father to whom the children will look for comfort and love. Although their demands, coupled with the stress of earning a living, may seem unbearable, children are desperately vulnerable at this point and need all the time a father can possible give.

The situation can be markedly different for a widower with teenage children. One man looked to his sixteen-year-old daughter to take over the household chores while he continued to do nothing in the house. She resented his demands because there were two younger children aged ten and thirteen in the family that had to be cared for. Her father expected her to do all the cooking, laundry, and cleaning because she was the eldest and a girl. He did not understand that it was a lot to ask of his daughter who had schoolwork to do and who wanted an active social life. It would have been more equitable if the father had split the chores up among himself and all the children. Failing that, he should have considered hiring a part-time housekeeper to help with the work.

Widowers often find they become closer to their children than ever before. It is important not to expect too much from them. They too have a great many changes to which they are forced to adjust. They cannot, for example, be expected to act as companions. Ultimately, they cannot help with their father's loneliness, particularly when they would prefer to be with their friends. They can, however, return the love and respect which a widowed father can give.

Unfortunately, some widowers run into difficulties when their children begin to leave home. Suddenly, faced with cooking and eating alone, washing their own laundry and cleaning house for themselves, they cannot adapt to a solitary life. Some men find this time such a painful one to endure that they lose the will to live and may, in fact, die shortly after their partner's death.

Many widowers, once they reach the point of being able to

accept their partner's death, find themselves sensing an emotional gap in their lives and may wish to remarry. As in the case of a widow remarrying, it is important to avoid being pushed into or out of a marital situation by family or friends. The decision is a very personal one and can be encouraged by the fact that second marriages are often more successful than first ones.

It is essential that all married couples realize that their partners could die at any time. No one is assured of living for any period of time at all, let alone to a ripe old age. While it would be folly to advocate total independence, each partner should avoid becoming completely tied to the other for survival. The answer lies in a healthy balance – a self-reliance which either partner can assume in the event of being left alone. Only through the awareness that any person can and may be left alone tomorrow, next week, or ten years from now, can one prepare in an adaptive way for that possibility.

IX
YOUR OWN DEATH

At some point in our lives each of us must come to terms with our own mortality. Although we are all aware that our lives are finite, reactions to thoughts of one's own death are largely governed by age.

For the young child, death represents isolation and separation from his parents. For the teenager death has a very different meaning. It is a cruel and bitter blow when one's life seems to be just beginning. For the young mother, impending death will likely generate concern over her husband and children, while a father may worry about his wife and her ability to earn a living or raise their family alone. Although there is great sadness and anger at dying so early, young parents tend to concentrate their concern on the family they leave behind.

As time passes and children grow and begin leading more independent lives, parents are no longer afraid that their deaths will prove devastating blows to the family. Rather, their concern is for their spouse. This period of so-called "middle age" is one in which many people re-evaluate their past life, their achievements and their relationships. If the re-evaluation proves satisfying, many people continue to enjoy life and not dwell to any extent on the fact that their life is probably about half over. Others, who are not satisfied with what they have accomplished, may panic and begin making impulsive changes in lifestyle in hopes of achieving some elusive dreams before their lives come to an end.

As people grow even older, entering their seventies and eighties, death is no longer as terrifying as it once was. On the contrary, the deaths of family and friends at this stage create an aura of familiarity, not fear, and many elderly people, too tired and worn to carry on, await death with a kind of quiet expectation.

In North American society the fear of death is widespread. It has become a taboo subject to which people often refer in terms of cautious euphemisms. People do not die in our society, they "pass away" or "pass on," not to the grave, but to a "final resting place." Because it is a difficult topic to discuss, many people are reluctant to talk about it or to confess their fears to others. One dying woman never told her husband about her own impending death because she was not supposed to know she was dying. Her husband knew, but did not want her told and she knew but was afraid her knowledge might upset her husband. As a result, everyone lived a gigantic lie, and she died without ever being able to express her fears.

Family participation in such cover-up situations is quite common, although a dying person is, in fact, rarely ignorant of his condition. Patients try to protect their families in the same way in which families try to protect dying patients, and so the hoax is perpetuated.

Although coming to term's with one's own mortality is a life long problem, many people wait until middle or old age to begin dealing with it. Unlike some problems which conveniently disappear if we ignore them, death is always with us and is much more easily dealt with earlier in life rather than later. Once a person is able to accept the limitations of his mortality, he has freed himself to get on with the process of living. Dealing with death, in later years, can become an obsession – it can permeate every aspect of life and be ready to surface at any moment in the mind of an elderly person. For example,

One man gathered his whole family together from across the country to celebrate his 75th birthday. When he stood up to give a speech, he started off by saying this was the last time he thought the whole family would be together before he died, and then gave detailed instructions about what he expected after his death. He wanted to be cremated and asked his wife that she spread his ashes over his favourite park. Needless to say the family was very upset to hear him talking this way and reassured him he would probably still live another twenty years.

Although, on a rational level, all people know that they will someday die, it is an incredible shock when a doctor confirms the presence of a fatal disease. Dr. Elisabeth Kubler-Ross has done some excellent work with people facing their own death and has written about the five stages through which most patients will pass in coming to terms with their own mortality. The initial diagnosis leads to shock and denial as the patient may have heard what the doctor said, but is not really ready to accept it yet.

Many people will try to offer some excuses such as, "They must have mixed up my lab results with some other patient's. It can't be me who is dying." If the doctor or family push the patient too hard at this stage, and break down the denial too soon, the patient can become panic stricken. Panic lies just behind denial, and the patient needs time to slowly face up to the truth.

Mrs. B. is dying of cancer, and some of her reactions to her disease illustrate how she is coming to terms with her own death. It all started twenty years ago when she was admitted to hospital to have a lump removed from her breast. She was twenty-six-years old at the time. She tells her story this way:

> No one told me that the lump might be malignant, and I received quite a shock when I woke up after my operation to find that both my breasts had been removed. I cried for days, because I felt like half a woman without any breasts. I had only been married two years earlier, and had a baby daughter at home. I never thought that this was going to lead to my death, and the only way I consoled myself was by thinking that although my breasts were gone, at least the disease was cured.
>
> Losing my breasts was quite an adjustment for me because

I was still a young woman and I wondered whether my husband would continue to find me sexually attractive. He was not as supportive as I would have liked and that marked the beginning of our marital problems.

During the next four years I completely blocked out the idea that I had had cancer, and never thought that I would have a recurrence. To my surprise, when I went to the doctor for a routine check-up, four years after the operation, he discovered a lump on one of my ovaries. Once again I was hospitalized, and I had to have my ovaries out. I was very frightened that the cancer might have spread, but the doctor assured me that it had not. He said I would be fine, and that once again I had beaten the cancer.

I allowed myself the luxury of believing I would be alright, and my husband helped my denial. He said, "You'll be fine. There's nothing to worry about." I guess it was easier to deny the cancer than to think that it might recur, so I blocked it from my mind once again. Life went on as usual. My little girl was growing up, and my husband and I managed to get along with one another day by day.

About five years later I had another recurrence, and had to have some lymph nodes removed. My doctor tended to gloss things over and didn't tell me the whole truth about my condition. I guess it must be very tough for doctors to deal with cancer patients because it can be such a terrible disease and people are so afraid of it. In my experience no one ever said the word cancer to me. It's always "growth" or "involvement." It's as if cancer were a four-letter word and shouldn't be mentioned by name.

Life went on as always. Some days were good, some were bad. I could no longer deny the fact that I had cancer but I was still avoiding thinking of death. The increased tensions in the household with my being sick deepened the rift between my husband and me. I guess our relationship had never been that good from the start, and it just deteriorated over the years.

Finally, three years ago, my husband left me. Our daughter was thirteen. He continued to send me money so that I was able to manage financially with him gone. My daughter was the only family I had left and I treasured her very much. I was very frightened of dying before she was old enough to look after herself.

When people no longer deny that they are sick and dying, they enter the stage of anger. This is the most dramatic stage of all. The patient will be angry at everyone and everything, and will say things such as – "Why me?" The dying person may get angry at the doctors and nurses, at friends and family, who remain healthy while the patient is losing everything.

Mrs. B. could no longer deny the truth about her cancer because it was beginning to wear her down physically.

All my life I had been very athletic and one day I decided that I was terribly out of shape. I thought jogging would help and I started running every night. I just didn't have the strength to run, and then I feared the worst. I went back to see the doctor and the next day I was back in hospital to have my adrenal glands taken out. I began to wonder how many parts of the body were dispensable.

Finally there was that day, a few months ago, when the doctor told me the cancer had invaded my bones and there was nothing more he could do for me. My initial reaction was one of blind fury. I started screaming at the doctor "For all these years you have been telling me you have it under control, and now this. What kind of a doctor are you anyhow?"

I ran out of his office and into a nearby park where I could sit down for a while. When I arrived at the park the sun was shining, the birds were singing, and there were dozens of university students all dressed in caps and gowns posing for photographs with proud parents. It was graduation day, and the park was filled with laughter and gaiety.

My anger and bitterness increased seeing all those happy healthy people when I had just found out I was going to die. Their laughter made me cry because I knew I would never be happy again, and I ran out of the park. All I could think of was why was this happening to me. I was still a young woman, and it just wasn't fair. Leaving the park, I saw an old drunk lying on a bench in a stupor, and I thought, "Why couldn't it be him, why does it have to be me?"

The third stage is one of bargaining. The dying person tries to make a truce in the hopes of averting death. He or she will offer anything to prevent death, may moderate demands and ask for just another few years, or even months. But the bargaining is an attempt to postpone the inevitable, and most bargains are directed toward God.

The fourth stage is one of depression. It is the time when the patient realizes that everything has failed: the medical treatment, the bargaining, the denial. At this stage there is no doubt in the person's mind that he or she is really dying. People realize that life is very different now. The past is over, there is little future left, there is only the present. This is the stage where people confront their lives and recount their achievements. They also think about the things they have not done, and realize it's too late to do anything about it. It is in this stage that people begin grieving for their own death, for it has suddenly become a reality.

When you lose a loved one you may become very depressed. When you are dying and losing everyone and everything, depression is inevitable. The fourth stage is a time when people like to be silent: they want to think about things. Idle chatter is no longer appreciated. What they are really doing in this stage is beginning to prepare for their separation, and this must be respected.

Mrs. B. went through this stage, and described her feelings this way:

> I'm still hanging on. The cancer has spread now: they tell me it is in one lung, and has invaded the bones in my rib cage. Some days I don't feel too bad. Other days I feel rotten. I sometimes wonder if all the pain is in my mind, because all along the doctors tried to make light of the disease. They never told me what I would probably experience, and I never knew what to expect next. I think they owe it to you as a human being to be more honest and

straightforward, but I guess maybe they're afraid of your reactions.

I started to panic when I finally knew my time was running out. There were so many things I wanted to achieve in my life that I had not even attempted. I always thought one day I would leave secretarial work to take up painting seriously. For years I considered myself an artist, but never found the time to devote myself to art. Now I knew that dream would never come true, because there just wasn't enough time. I started thinking about the lousy relationship I had with my husband and realized that I would never experience a true and deep love relationship with a man. I became very sad when I knew it was over for me. I had my chance and I blew it. There were so many things I wanted to do, and so many places I wanted to visit, but it was too late.

Another depressing thing for me was that the cancer was beginning to affect me physically more and more. I have slowed down in the last year and that has been hard to take. I know I will not be able to take my annual skiing trip this winter because I no longer have the strength.

The final stage in facing one's own death is acceptance. The dying person has worked his way through the other stages and looks to his own death with quiet expectation. All that is left now is the waiting. There is almost a feeling of self-reliance in this stage because dying people no longer have great needs. They sometimes pull back from other people, which may be hard for family and friends to understand. This stage is a mellow one and is not filled with the dramatic emotions of the previous stages. Not all dying people reach this final stage. Some never stop struggling and never resign themselves to impending death. Mrs. B. has reached this final stage:

In the last few weeks I have gotten over the initial panic I felt when I knew I was going to die. I realize that if I have not done certain things until now, they are really not that important to me. I don't want to take a trip around the world because it would mean leaving my family and close friends behind. Life has become much more simplified for me now. I live for the moment and enjoy each day as much as I possibly can.

If I had to say what the most important thing in life was I would say relationships with people. Money, possessions and power which people value so much are not important to me. People are important. Families are important. If everyone who was healthy could learn that little secret I have to share, they would learn life's most important lesson.

I think I have accepted my death. It doesn't frighten me anymore. I'm afraid that my daughter has not yet faced the truth about my fate. She talks about the future together when I know there is no future for me. I am thankful that I have my daughter to look after me, because I know it will become more and more difficult for me to look after myself. She just got engaged to a very nice guy, and I can now rest more easily knowing she won't be alone when I'm gone. I feel sad for my daughter who will have to watch me getting worse and finally dying.

My one great fear is that I will die alone, in an undignified way, with tubes inserted in my body and all sorts of mechanical devices that I don't want. Death itself doesn't scare me. I look upon it as going to sleep and being in peace after a long fight. I would like to die at home with my daughter at my bedside because I want her face to be the last vision I have in my life. She is my stake in the future, and I believe I will live on through her.

Sometimes I think about that day I found out I was going to die. I remember going into the park and being angry at all those graduating students for being happy and healthy. Then I remember that I came to the same park with my parents when my brother graduated from university twenty years ago. We were all filled with the same pride and joy that day. It made me realize that life goes on.

Students and parents will be coming to the same park to celebrate graduations for many years to come. People are born and die every minute, but life goes on as always. I realize that my daughter will be sad when I'm gone, and so will some of my friends, but apart from that, nothing will have changed.

Mrs. B. has finally come to terms with her own impending death. She is no longer depressed or angry, but is resigned to the fact that these are her last months. Her daughter, on the other hand, is still denying the finality of her mother's cancer. Mrs. B. has read a couple of good books written by cancer patients which she has offered to lend her daughter, but her daughter cannot bring herself to read them. Because her mother is the only close family she has, Miss B. cannot bear the pain of facing up to her death.

When people think about their own death they often envisage exotic holidays or some other "final fling." In this last stage, however, most dying people want very ordinary things – to see those who are closest to them, to play favourite records and to go for walks. Most of all they want to be with those people around whom they feel most comfortable. These relationships are, in the final analysis, our most prized possessions.

How the Dying Person Interacts With Other People

The way the dying person reacts to the people around him will depend on which of the five stages he is in. If he is still denying the diagnosis, he will feel comforted if other people tell him he will get better soon. If he is in the angry stage he may blow up at the friend who says he will get better soon, and may say, "That's easy for you to say – you don't have to die soon." If he is depressed, he may react to the same comment by falling even further into despair. He knows he will never get better, and cannot share the denial with his friends. If the dying person has reached the stage of acceptance, nothing his friends say to him will really matter because he is at peace with the world, and has accepted his fate.

In general, dying people do not want to be treated differently from everyone else. They are happiest with people who don't put on a happy face, but are just themselves. Mrs. B. found some of her friends could cope quite well, while others couldn't. She said:

Some of my friends have been marvellous to me. They want to help me if they can, and they want to know what I am going through. For a person dying of cancer as I am, denial is no help. What I want from people is that they acknowledge the fact that I have cancer and not pretend there is a cure.

Each person is different though. One friend is very nervous when she comes to see me, and I can tell she is afraid of knowing the truth about me. I have to comfort her, and have to pretend that things aren't too bad with me. I have another friend whose visits I appreciate much more because I can really be myself with him.

One day I was feeling very blue, and started crying in front of him. He looked me straight in the eye and said, "O.K., we both know you have cancer, but you're not going to die today, so what's the problem?" That was the best thing he could have done for me. I snapped out of my depression and stopped feeling sorry for myself. Whenever I get down I remember his words, "You're not going to die today," and that helps me a lot.

It's hard for dying people to tell other people they are dying because of the reactions they get. Most people are shocked and don't know where to look or what to say. Mrs. B. tried to avoid telling people she had cancer because of the reactions she got from them. However, she did have one experience which was exactly the opposite, and it made her day:

I could not work for a while during some treatments which made me feel unwell. I went to apply for unemployment insurance and the young girl who interviewed me asked why I could not work. She pressed me to tell her what was wrong with me, but I was reluctant because of my past negative experiences with telling strangers the truth. She continued to ask me, and finally I said, "I have cancer."

Her eyes opened wide, and she replied, "Do you really? Isn't that interesting! I've been reading a lot about cancer recently, but have never actually met anyone who had it. You look well, how do you feel?" Her innocent curiosity and spontaneity delighted me and I said to her, "I wish more people would be like you instead of just turning their heads away and saying 'I'm sorry.' ''

It can be very difficult for the friends of the dying person to know what to do or say when death is near. Being with a dying person is also a reminder of our own mortality. One of Mrs. B.'s friends told me that he had a frightening dream one night. He dreamt Mrs. B. was close to death and asked him to hold her hand while she died. Instead of remaining with her he turned and ran because he was unable to stay and watch her die. Remember that it is very lonely to die and no one wants to die alone.

Some people seem to be able to consciously postpone their own death by exerting what doctors often refer to as the will to live. This will is sometimes so strong that people who are close to death may miraculously recover. On the other hand, some patients appear to lose this will to live and simply stop fighting. A doctor working with an elderly man who was dying described this most dramatic case:

> Although the disease was irreversible he was determined he wasn't going to give up. He was prepared to go on living with his disease as long as he knew there were pain killers to help get him through the day. This man treasured life so much he felt it was certainly worth hanging on to, even at a high price.

> When he became progressively worse, at the final stages of his illness, I had to leave him. I was rescheduled to go on a long- planned holiday with my wife and children which I felt I could not cancel. I apologized to him that I had to leave at this time, but he understood that I had a commitment to my family. Before I left he said to me, "Don't worry about me because I'll be here when you get back in two weeks." I doubted it very much because he was very ill and most of his systems had virtually ceased functioning.

> When I returned, two weeks later, to my amazement he was still alive. I went into his room and the first thing he said, "I told you I'd still be here." He said very little to me the next two days and was dead 48 hours after my return.

The will to live varies tremendously from person to person, but is often closely associated with a patient's personality. Those who have found life burdensome, at best, often give up quickly, while those who have found life stimulating and pleasurable are often reluctant to let go. It is a marvellous example of how the human mind and body interact. While man cannot conquer death, he can sometimes prolong life.

While we all live our lives in the knowledge that no day can be repeated and that we cannot alter the past, many of us are reluctant to plan for death – the inevitable termination of life. There are a number of very practical measures which can be taken that help, not only to prepare ourselves, but also to assure some security for those left behind. Everyone should have a will which can be updated periodically as commitments and financial situations change. This will ensure that the appropriate people will be provided for even in the event of an accidental death.

Dealing with one's own death is probably the most difficult task anyone will ever have to face. It means giving up everything and everyone of value in a lifetime. The knowledge of one's own impending death necessitates an awesome adjustment both in terms of personal feelings and in relationships with others. A patient should be prepared for the stages that precede acceptance – denial, anger, bargaining and depression. Some people find themselves stuck at one stage and needing help to overcome it. Family, friends, and doctors can help. No one need suffer in silence. Dying is a lonely and painful experience and entitles the patient to all the care and comfort available.

A dying person may find his family using a great deal of denial and false reassurance. It is important to understand that they are just trying to help. They may not be able to face the truth themselves and are, with good intentions, trying to protect the patient as well. If a dying person can be honest with himself and his family the energy normally expended in keeping up a facade can be diverted towards a few weeks or months of enjoyment of one another. The final months need not be gloomy and dark. Many people choose to remain at home surrounded by familiar and comfortable people and objects. It is a time to enjoy each day as a precious gift, to enjoy doing those things which bring the most pleasure and satisfaction and to tell family and friends how much one really cares about them.

What comes after death is very much an enigma. While varying cultures and religions hold a variety of beliefs, the only certainty is that each one of us lives on through our children and the other people we leave behind. Our ultimate immortality comes, in fact, with our own death which gives way to new life through our children and our grandchildren.

X
SUICIDE AND THE SURVIVORS

While suicide actually accounts for less than two deaths per hundred in Canada and the United States, certain alarming trends have become apparent. The rate among young people, for example, has risen drastically, more than tripling in the fifteen to twenty-four age group in the last twenty years. More women than men, in fact twice as many, attempt suicide, but twice as many men as women actually succeed in killing themselves. The most vulnerable, of course, are those who are "unattached" – single, divorced, widowed – those who are not settled in any kind of close relationship.

The kinds of feelings which envelop a potential suicide victim are of a depth and intensity which very few people can ever experience, much less understand. Often, too, the feelings which precipitate a suicide attempt may be resolved by the attempt itself. Women, for example, will sometimes attempt suicide when an affair or a marriage has disintegrated.

These attempted suicides, however, are often not serious. They are really attempts to hurt or punish another person and once that has been accomplished the suicidal feelings are usually satisfied. Many more attempted suicides are simply cries for help. This is often the case with young people who are desperately craving attention from family and friends and who have simply run out of time and energy.

Needless to say, suicide threats should never be ignored. They are rarely uttered for the sake of stimulating conversation. They are a clear statement about the depth of an individual's unhappiness and helplessness and the underlying pleas for help must be faced and resolved. Suicidal feelings are unpredictable at best, and should never be underestimated. An attempt at suicide may be the only way in which a depressed person can actually prove the depth of this feeling.

A husband may say to his wife, "I'm very depressed. Things are going so badly for me and I sometimes think suicide is the only answer." A response such as, "Oh, come on now, perk up. Things aren't that bad," will likely only make him angrier and he may feel obliged to prove the extent of his depression. The answer should be, "If you really do feel that badly, maybe you need to get help, or maybe we should both get help. Why don't we talk about it."

Because suicidal feelings are generally viewed by outsiders with substantial uncertainty and great distaste, the potential victim feels isolated. People simply choose not to talk about suicide, particularly with an individual who is giving the whole matter fairly serious consideration. It makes them uncomfortable and they often resort to an, "Oh, come on. Don't be silly," kind of attitude which only compounds the sadness of the person involved. He becomes convinced that no one has ever experienced similar feelings, that he is insane or that he will never be happy again. This is not a time for the home remedies of family or friends. It is essential that any person who feels suicidal be placed immediately in the care of a professional, who can listen with objectivity and heal with patience and trust.

For the person who actually does commit suicide, the reasons can be innumerable and are usually very complex. Often a problem relationship is compounded by a secondary problem such as drinking, depression, unemployment or illness. For men, being unable to support their families, being arrested for a crime, or suffering some other loss of self-respect may create pressures which cannot be resolved.

People sometimes use suicide as a means of resolving an inability to deal with the death of another close individual, perhaps a mother, father, or sibling. Studies have shown that suicide can follow a pattern and very often runs in families. Often the study of a suicide victim will reveal a similar pattern in preceding generations, with individuals often choosing the same method and time of suicide as a parent or grandparent.

The effects of suicide on the survivors (the child, sibling, or parent of someone who has killed himself) while perhaps not immediately visible, can be immeasurable, particularly if no attempt is made to resolve the suicide immediately. The people who suffer most in the family after the suicide of a parent are the children. They are the least involved in what is happening and yet, at the same time, they have to deal with all the negative feelings surrounding the death. Very often the cause of death is kept a mystery, an aura of secrecy surrounds the dead person and conflicting stories are rampant. Thus it is inevitable that children are left in a kind of limbo – confused and unable to distinguish fact from fantasy.

Many of the physical aspects of the stress are fairly common – insomnia, stomachaches, headaches, unruly behaviour, and problems at school. Underlying these symptoms, however, are the real problems. Children of suicide victims often shoulder a tremendous burden of guilt and believe that they were in some way responsible for the parent's death and were, in fact, negligent in failing to prevent it.

Ten year old Mike wanted desperately to go to summer camp but his parents refused. Mike's mother had been depressed for some time and wanted the child to be with her over the summer. Mike resented being away from his friends and disliked the depressing atmosphere at home and his mother's moodiness. His father, however, insisted that he stay at home and try to avoid antagonizing his mother. Then, one day, Mike found his mother lying dead in the living room.

His immediate reaction was to assume the entire responsibility for her death. Had she done it because she knew he was angry at not going to camp? Had he, in fact, antagonized her to the point of "craziness?" Mike was so tortured by his own guilt feelings and his father's reaction, "Why didn't you look after her?" that he became completely unable to function at school. Only when Mike's teacher called did his father realize the extent to which his son harbored responsibility for the suicide. His father recognized the problem and sought professional help immediately, so that Michael eventually came to realize that he was not connected with his mother's death and that his father did not blame him.

Sometimes the surviving parent expends considerable energy in convincing the children (and others) that the death was not suicide at all. Questions may be avoided and factual evidence blatantly contradicted. Friends who know the truth and relatives who enjoy discussing the death are avoided. In extreme cases families will move to a new city where hopefully no one will know or speculate about their background.

Obviously, this pattern of behaviour on the part of the surviving parent can have a devastating effect on the children's ability to deal with reality. It is virtually impossible for children to face and accept truths if no one else does. This twisting of or avoidance of reality leaves children filled with distrust. They are unable to distinguish what is real from what is not. In addition, these misguided attempts to protect children and to cover up the shame and guilt can often completely stultify the normal mourning process. It is impossible to express grief in such a contrived setting and the grieving process is often left incomplete. Lingering depression frequently substitutes for this unfinished mourning and can quickly become a way of life unless the family can deal with it quickly in an honest and open way.

Colin, a thirty-year-old man whom I treated, had a great deal of difficulty in coming to terms with his father's suicide, primarily because it was the culmination of the family's long term problems:

> My father, who was a prominent physicist, committed suicide two years ago, and even now virtually no one outside the family knows it was suicide. He went to England to spend a holiday with some relatives, but was very anxious

that my mother stayed at home. Just before he was due to arrive home my mother received a call from the police which said that he had disappeared. About two weeks later his body washed ashore. A lawyer in the family attempted to have the death certificate altered, but to no avail. The subsequent inquest showed that he had taken an overdose of barbiturates and after leaving his car and personal belongings on the beach, had simply walked in to the sea.

We learned shortly afterwards, that he had attempted suicide at least once before. Just a couple of months before his death he had taken an overdose at home but was rushed to hospital. My mother, of course, hushed it up saying he was having heart problems and nothing more was said.

Colin's father left no suicide note, but Colin was later able to piece together some clues to help him understand. His father was sixty-four years old and had been the head of research at the same firm for about fifteen years. He did, in fact, have heart problems which could have been corrected by surgery. However he kept postponing it and seemed unduly worried that an operation might incapacitate him. In addition, Colin learned about a meeting of department heads in the company which was scheduled to take place after his father's holiday. One of the topics for discussion was his position as Head of Research, which was apparently in jeopardy. As Colin said:

I think one of the reasons he killed himself was that he could not face retirement. There were other things too. His health wasn't particularly good and he was very depressed about it. His behaviour became very moody and erratic in the last few years, but the change was so gradual that I guess none of us paid much attention.

When we opened the safe after he died we found all kinds of drugs. I guess he was a drug addict which would certainly help to explain his behaviour. He used to do strange things, wearing outrageous clothes, taking a sleeping bag to an art gallery in case he wanted to sleep, ordering coffee in a chic restaurant, then pulling out a bag of bologna sandwiches to eat along with the coffee. I used to think he behaved in an eccentric way just to get attention.

His other method of attracting attention was to demand immediate action in garages, restaurants, clubs, and banks – he created a scene by shrieking at waiters, clerks, and tellers until he got his own way. I suppose now that this whole pattern of behaviour probably followed his increasing use of drugs, but we all just turned a blind eye and continued to convince ourselves that he was just being eccentric.

He didn't used to be eccentric though. I had a very orderly and proper upbring, with a strict father who was always the boss. Any personal discussion about thoughts or feelings simply didn't occur, and the dinner conversation always revolved around the government, socialism, and the economy. We all played along with it.

My mother came from a "good" family and was, of course, well versed in all the social niceties, but that was all she had going for her. Her idea of family life was to have everybody together at Christmas and Easter. There was a lot of hugging and kissing, and a lot of back- stabbing after the festivities were over.

In our family everything was measured on two levels. One was money, and the other was the level of achievement. As long as things were going well on those two levels everything was fine. But as soon as there was any trouble my parents didn't want to have any part of it. I once got eighty-five in chemistry and my father wanted to hire a tutor to help me improve my marks.

The real problem arose when I failed French in my third year at university. My father's reaction was to call me a failure and order me out of the house. I began to feel that I probably was a failure and would never be able to live up to anyone's expectations of me. I was confused, but because my parents denied the fact that there was any problem, I really had no one to turn to for help.

My way of dealing with it and of getting back at my parents, I guess was to try and commit suicide. I took an overdose, but not enough to kill me. I just wanted someone to listen to me. It didn't work though. My parents were so good at denial that they simply convinced themselves that there was no problem. I was still all alone.

This family's entire existence was based on visible success and financial security. There was no room for the expression of any emotion and no sharing of a member's problems. The atmosphere at home was, needless to say, a highly volatile one and when Dr. L. sensed failure in his job he solved it alone. It was impossible for him to discuss his fears and loss of pride with his wife and sons, simply because the family had never been a source of comfort and caring for its members.

After Dr. L.'s death, Colin's problems began to intensify. There was no real sadness over his father's death, but rather a feeling of tremendous guilt at not feeling sad. Colin's guilt was confused by other thoughts as well. One was that now he was finally free of his father's expectations for him. The other was a very real sense of hurt at having been deprived of a decent father-son relationship. His feelings were terribly confused at this point, partly because feelings were so alien to his upbringing and also because he sensed that it was wrong to have unpleasant and angry thoughts about people who have died.

His mixed feelings were very natural, of course. But it was many months before Colin was able to accept his anger at not feeling loved by his father and his disappointment at being abandoned by him. Colin's mother, on the other hand, has never been able to accept her husband's abandonment and is able to live with it only by idealizing it. Colin described it in this way:

> During the two years since my father's suicide, my mother has distorted the event so much that she now refers to his death as the ultimate act of courage. Her own guilt will never allow her to face the truth. She must have known that he would probably try suicide on the trip to England, particularly since he was so anxious to have her stay at home. She knew, but she did nothing. As far as she is concerned, no one beyond the immediate family knows the truth.

I have never even heard her use the word suicide, and although it appears to be a well-kept secret, I am sure lots of people who knew him were suspicious. I think, though, that because she has told so many people that he had a heart attack she almost believes her own lie.

After the suicide strange things began happening to me. I began acting in the same erratic and temperamental way my father used to act. That, I guess, is the ultimate irony. After the tremendous relief and realization that with my father dead I could live my own life, I found I was still bound to him after all. I still had all of my father's expectations inside me. I wasn't enjoying life, and I was terrified that I might attempt suicide again and succeed.

Finally my wife insisted I see a psychiatrist. I had so many problems to work out: my own background, my expectations of myself as opposed to those of my family, and, of course, my father's suicide. Now, three years later, I think I have made the most important discovery about my life, that families are for sharing and that people really can help each other if they can be honest and not afraid to ask.

Dr. L.'s suicide and the aftermath provide a tragic example of a superficially successful family which had no established pattern for sharing and resolving the problems of its members. As a result, problems were isolated in a vacuum with no perspective and no experience with which to view them. Dr. L., who was deeply disturbed in the last years before his death, did not want help from anyone.

After his first suicide attempt, which combined with his erratic behaviour should have brought drastic action from his family, his wife denied any problem. Dr. L. flatly refused his own son's advice to see a psychiatrist because he was unaccustomed to seeking outside help. After the suicide, when Mrs. L. must have been overwhelmed by her role in it, she chose to cover up the whole event by denial. In that way she postponed, probably forever, facing her own guilt.

Colin, as a product of this bizarre household, had no hope of enjoying a problem-free life. This inability to face problems and the ease with which they could be "covered up" was so much a part of his upbringing that he was unable to function any other way. It was when Colin's behaviour began to appear remarkably like his father's, however, that his wife confronted him with the situation. She demanded that he seek help as the only alternative to destroying his family as his father had done. Colin was extremely fortunate in being able to use his experiences in terms of his own personal growth. Many suicide survivors unfortunately fail to acknowledge the fact that their own lives may require a great deal of analysis and restructuring.

Certainly the impact of suicide on the survivors is a dramatic one, but it is perhaps even more so for the surviving spouse. This is because the death brings not only the normal feelings of losing someone close, but also forces the spouse to appraise the causes and his or her guilt in a unique way. "Why didn't I foresee and prevent it?" "Wasn't I a good husband or wife?" "Was I responsible?" "Was he trying to punish me?" These are all questions which may run through the survivor's mind in trying to understand what happened.

Those who have had a good relationship with the victim have the best chance of resolving these conflicts quickly. Those who had a precarious relationship may find it more difficult to resolve their roles in the death. It is perfectly normal to feel rejected and to wonder why the victim did not ask for help. It is just as natural to feel disillusioned with a husband or wife for not having the strength to go on living, or to feel angry at having been abandoned. These feelings can be remarkably intense, particularly in the first few weeks after the death.

The surviving spouse must also be prepared to deal with the blame and often the gossip perpetrated by friends and relatives. This too is natural. Suicide makes people feel uncomfortable and attempts to justify the death are often little more than attempts to come to terms with the death and be rid of the embarrassment and shame with comments such as, "Their marriage wasn't very good anyway," or, "She drove him to it, you know."

In addition, it is often difficult to form new relationships after a close relationship with a suicide victim. The hurt and rejection may be transformed into distrust and a lack of self-confidence even though the survivor wants desperately to be close to someone again. Often conversations with a close friend, priest, rabbi, or a psychiatrist can re-establish the survivor's trust and self-worth and encourage the formation of new bonds.

Finally, one of the very real dangers is that the survivor may follow the suicide pattern. Mr. and Mrs. C. had a very precarious marriage and had, in fact, married only because Mrs. C. was pregnant. Their fifteen-year-old son was the only reason that the marriage had remained intact. When the son shot himself and died both parents were deeply disturbed. Because they did not have a marriage in which each partner helped the other, the tragedy did not bring them closer together. It drove them apart.

Mr. C. went to visit his son's grave almost every day and said over and over again that he had nothing to live for. Mrs. C. blamed herself for being a poor mother, but kept all her feelings to herself. She began spending more and more time with her parents who denied her the opportunity to talk about what happened, and who tried to convince her that fresh air and regular meals were all that were needed to speed her recovery.

About three months later Mr. C. shot himself in the same room and with the same gun which his son had used. His suicide note read, "Life isn't worth living anymore. I want to be with Jimmy again. There's nothing left for me on earth." Mrs. C. found her husband exactly as she had found her son. She was now completely alone. She has been so traumatized by both suicides that she will likely never recover. She has become suicidal herself and despite intensive psychotherapy has not been able to overcome her depression. Unless she can find a new purpose in her life there is a distinct danger that she too will kill herself.

There is no harm in dwelling on the suicide so long as the results are therapeutic. "Did the victim give clues which were ignored?" "Was the victim rejected through cruelty or lack of love?" "Was the child or spouse degraded and stripped of any sense of self-worth?" "Was each achievement never quite enough?" Pondering these questions will not bring back the suicide victim, but may provide some useful information to the survivors who may need therapy either individually or as a group.

Families must remember, however, that they cannot and should not assume all the responsibility for what happens to their members.   Unknown frustrations from school and friends, or impulsive spur-of- the-moment acts are beyond the control of most families. Whatever the reasons, there comes a point at which the survivors must stop looking solely at the victim and look as well at themselves. They must begin to mourn the dead one, to reshape their own lives, to work out their own degrees of responsibility and to recognize and change the destructive patterns that may be present in their own lives and relationships.

If someone in a family has committed suicide it is essential that the survivors do not attempt to "cover it up" as an accident or as foul play. Difficult as it may be, the death must be faced for exactly what it is. Any distortion of the truth means living a perpetual lie and few people have either the energy or the stability to carry it through. Talking is not the whole answer, but it is a beginning.

For children, talking is extraordinarily important as they may be less well equipped than adults to deal with their feelings. Their questions must be answered, no matter how painful or difficult. This is probably their first exposure to suicide and they will need reassurance that they were not responsible and that no one else will abandon them in the same way. Unfortunately, our society has no rituals for dealing with suicide. Its taboo nature has deprived survivors of even the capacity to talk about it.

One widow spoke to her priest about her intense sense of shame after her husband's suicide. The priest advised her not to tell anyone what caused his death, and she invented a story about an accident which she then reported to friends and family. She managed to maintain her pledge of silence for almost a year, despite enormous guilt, fear and loneliness; but eventually she confided in a friend. This sharing of her pain with someone else gave her an immense sense of relief and greatly helped her begin to accept and deal with the truth. The ideal situation, of course, would be an organization for families who have experienced suicide (similar to groups for widows) where they can share their concerns and challenge their problems.

Survivors of suicide frequently tell of feelings of relief and anger after the victim's death. Because these kinds of feelings towards the dead are considered inappropriate, attempts are often made to suppress them by falsely idolizing the dead person or by inventing excuses to explain the suicide. This may cover up the survivor's feelings of rejection and abandonment on the surface, but will not resolve the true feelings in the long term. They are to be examined as openly and honestly as possible, if the process of mourning is to begin in earnest.

It is important to remember that despite the cause of death the suicide victim deserves the one universal ritual of death – that of saying goodbye. While families often prefer private funerals in the case of suicide, there are often many other people, relatives and distant friends, who are anxious to say goodbye as well.

The bereaved family also needs all the kindness and caring that would be expressed if the death had been a heart attack or a car accident. The bereaved appreciate genuine expressions of caring and affection even if it is impossible to know what to say, and sometimes even more awkward to say it. A simple note which indicates a desire to share in the sorrowing is always welcomed and often cherished.

Because suicide seems to be so senseless it is doubly hard for those left behind. Suicide is not a "neat and tidy" way to die, for it inevitably creates enormous anxiety and guilt in the immediate survivors and innumerable questions and speculation on the part of interested bystanders. Suicide is unique in that its victims can consciously choose to live or die, and the complexities of death by suicide involve the survivors as much as, if not more than, the victim. For many of the survivors a suicide can be the beginning of the end. For many more however, who are open and honest in their appraisals of themselves and in their relationships with both the living and the dead, it can be another beginning.

XI
The Way It Is

The death of a loved one provides many individuals with the opportunity to evaluate the quality of their own lives at a time when grief reminds us of the fragility and preciousness of our own existence. The void left by the loss of a family member can also serve as the beginning of a re-evaluation of our lives.

There are many ways for a person to live his or her life, paths that are chosen but nevertheless influenced by a myriad of factors. The cultural, economic, racial, and religious background of an individual are all significant elements that shape one's development; however, they do not entirely determine how we live our lives. We must also find a way to cope with a world that is often characterized by evil and ugliness. In doing so, we must make the choices and value judgements that test the scope of our own realms of experience. Decency characterizes individuals who are raised in a family setting where love, respect, and trust are cultivated and each person is allowed the freedom to make decisions that will sustain his or her own selfhood without destroying others. In reflecting upon death, either the passing of a loved one or the end of one's own life, the desire to find merit in how an individual's life had been lived is a difficult and inevitable process. Mortality reminds us that there is a circularity to life that limits one's opportunities but, conversely, allows a reassessment of one's achievements and the possibility of change. The question of how we live our lives becomes crucial as the search for success in life is refashioned by an awareness of our own mortality and the mortality of those around us.

In my years of treating a wide variety of patients who have
had to face death, or through the death of a relative, spouse,
child or friend, the issue of integrity is a recurring theme.
However, this integrity, or ability to give back to society rather
than destroying others, has some particularly relevant mani-
festations within dysfunctional families, where the death of an
individual leaves a void that cannot be filled by positive, living
memories. Instead, such deaths perpetuate destruction, the
burden of which placed on the remaining family members.

One patient I treated, David, was raised in a highly dysfunctional family. His father was a well-respected physician
whose facade of financial and social success, hid the severity of
his depressions, destroying any semblance of a father-son
bond. David's mother ignored her husband's illness, determined to maintain her status and marriage despite the damage that was inflicted by her husband upon both her and her
son. When I first saw David, his father had just committed
suicide, an act that had both shocked and horrified his family.
Yet, his mother refused to discuss the death with David, insist-
ing that it was merely an accident. Unfortunately, David's
memories of his father were characterized by the craziness
with which he functioned in his daily life, a destructiveness
that encompassed David. As David explains, "I was never
praised by my father for anything that I did. It was always a
question of what I could have done better." Furthermore,
David had never been shown any affection, a result of a background which did not allow for emotional exchanges. Thus,
the self-centredness of father's life, which only included his
needs, left permanent scars on his family even after his death.

The death of David's father marked a critical point in
David's life, a chance to potentially re-evaluate the impact of
his father's destructive attitude on his own life. David also had
the opportunity to examine the course of his own life and to
consider whether he was following his father's poor example
within the context of his family. Importantly, David had come
to see me at his wife's urging because she suspected that he,

like his father, was depressed. David's wife was struggling to understand her husband's selfishness and lack of interest in his children. Moreover, David had begun to threaten suicide on a regular basis, often telling his wife that he was going out for a drive and never coming back. David's own repetition of his father's behavioral patterns indicated an unhealthy response to his death, an attitude that needed to be treated and changed.

The complexity of David's response to his father's death raises several questions about the impact of death on individuals. In David's case, although the death of his father provided an opportunity to re-evaluate his own behaviour, he was unable to seize the chance to release himself from the past. David's mother's denial over the details of the suicide, largely out of social concerns, did not allow David to express his hatred and subsequent grief for his father to his mother. Instead, David engaged in the same tactics that his father had to maintain power over the family structure. He held his family "up for ransom" by threatening to kill himself. Thus, death, for David, became a tool with which he was able to manipulate those around him. This manifestation of David's cruelty after the death of his father was a reaction to his death but one that lacked the integrity and respect that characterizes normal families who go through the grieving process. When a societal or familial conscience is lacking within the family structure from generation to generation and no alternative models are provided, where can an individual like David turn? The opportunity to find love, trust, and the chance to develop as a healthy person were eroded to such a degree in David's case because his father's death perpetuated in him the self centredness that had destroyed his father.

In talking to David's children, I realized that David's repeated suicide threats were also altering their understanding of death and dying in a negative and potentially dangerous manner. The children, a boy aged eight and a girl aged six, told me that their father played games with them when he threatened suicide and that they could no longer take him seriously, a reaction that suggested the children's inability to see past the notion of death as a power structure or game. Moreover, the boy, Ryan, stated that "My father doesn't love me anyway so what does it matter if he dies. . ." The cruelty that had been inflicted on David throughout his childhood and adolescence was echoed in this statement by Ryan, indicating the impact of David's own upbringing on the lives of his children. Thus, death for David's children was devalued both as a point of loss and re- evaluation in the lives of the survivors. The self respect that David sought and could not find in remembering his father after his suicide, was perpetuated by David's own behaviour toward his family.

The suicide or death of a family member who has inflicted cruelty and selfishness on his or her family creates a dilemma for the survivors, a problem that both David and his children raised throughout their discussions with me. David was caught between the relief he felt over his father's suicide and a sense of love for a man who had never shown any love for him; hatred and guilt were central to this dilemma in David's case. Similarly, David's children expressed feelings of remorse and anger toward their father's repeated suicide threats. A sense of abandonment also characterized both David and his children; however, due to the dysfunctional structure of the family, this feeling of loss was not countered with any kind of happy memories or strong bonds that could allow for the survivors to recover emotionally. In David's case, even after his father's suicide, David's father remained present in the family. His ability to wield power over the family, acting in a cruel and selfish manner, was reflected through his choosing to commit suicide, thereby leaving the family to pick up the pieces after his death. David's own behaviour toward his children, namely his suicide threats, reflected the same inability to act with decency and perpetuated precisely the same dilemma that father had presented to him.

In treating David and his family, it was essential to examine the issue of integrity because David was deprived of the love, trust and respect that characterizes healthy families. Thus he was also denied the chance to recover his self-esteem after his father's suicide. This inability to cope with death was then manifested in David's cruelty toward his own children, a perpetuation of the same tragedy displayed by previous generations. Without the normal mechanisms that allow family members to grieve, reminisce and re-evaluate life and mortality, death becomes simply another mechanism of destruction for both the deceased and those who are left behind. It was necessary for David to assess his own behaviour toward his family in light of his father's treatment of himself. Furthermore, David had to consider how his own cruelty and selfishness had devalued the significance of death in his children's eyes; the constant threats of suicide placed an inappropriate and unhealthy emphasis on death, leaving the children with feelings of fear, remorse and confusion over their father's potential actions. It was necessary for David to see how cruel behaviour would result in harm to several generations, a pattern that would have to be reversed in order to salvage his children's self-esteem and give them a healthy understanding of mortality.

David's case reflects one specific instance of the harm that occurs when a death takes place within a dysfunctional family. The cruelty and selfishness that characterize the actions of several generations, both in life and death, can have particularly severe and lasting consequences. Yet, there are other instances where reflection on the process of death and dying are both significant and instructive. A patient whom I treated several years ago was a middle-aged woman with five children who had been diagnosed with inoperable lung cancer and who came to see me on the advice of a family friend. Unlike David and his father who viewed death as a tool of power with which to manipulate the family, Susan was a talented professional, a loving wife and mother, whose diagnosis was an unexpected and devastating event in her life. Although Susan knew she was dying, she chose not to discuss this painful discovery with either friends or family in any detail, and she struggled in particular to shield her children from her illness. Susan, in clinical terms, was exhibiting signs of denial, and an unwillingness to prepare herself and her family for her death. While the "will to live" often sustains terminally ill patients, allowing them to postpone death and accomplish important goals within their lives, Susan's denial concerned me. She expressed incredible guilt over "abandoning her children" but, by refusing to discuss her illness with them and make adequate preparations for this eventuality, Susan was unable to address that which most concerned her. Moreover, Susan's husband was unwilling to acknowledge his wife's cancer and to deal with the possibility of losing her. By surrounding Susan with silence, her husband did not help her deal with her disease nor to cope with her mortality.

Although the issue of death in Susan's case was not plagued with the same selfishness and cruelty of David's family, the silence that surrounds the mortality of all of us remains a significant problem both for the person who is dying and those who are left behind. Though Susan's life reflected a great deal of success from her own perspective, her refusal to talk about her illness made it difficult for her to achieve the things she wanted to in the time that remained. Susan talked about her love for her children and her desire for them not to feel abandoned when she passed away; yet she would not broach the topic of death, even with her eldest son who at the age of 13 was aware of the seriousness of his mother's illness and wanted to know what was going on. The decency that characterized Susan's life, her love and caring for her family, did not alleviate her unhealthy reaction to her own death because, by hiding her cancer, she was unable to allow herself and those around her, to come to terms with her death. The silence that Susan exhibited toward family members and friends, like David's mother, suggested her unwillingness to deal with the reality of her own mortality. In treating Susan, I urged her to reconsider the steps she was taking to shield others from her cancer, as her ability to help her family cope with the loss and her own peace of mind depended upon frank and honest discussions about death and dying.

Death and the fear of dying pose unique challenges to every individual, a coming to terms with mortality that can produce positive and sustained results when a healthy attitude is taken toward this process. Although many of the patients who come to see me suffer from the burden of a dysfunctional family or the desire to deny death, others find the strength and courage to make enormous contributions to the communities in which they live, despite their suffering. One woman in particular, a patient named Ruth, embodies the kind of integrity that allows families to cope with death. Ruth was diagnosed with breast cancer in her late 30's, at a time in her life when her career as a journalist was flourishing. Ruth came to see me at her husband's urging because of the severe depression she suffered following her diagnosis. As she explained to me, "My body has taken over my life. I am too sick to work or to do anything. I feel trapped." Ruth faced a double mastectomy and her doctor had warned her that there was a very good chance that the cancer would spread, a situation that would dramatically alter her life.

Initially in treating Ruth, we spent a great deal of time discussing the impact of the cancer on her family, an issue that concerned her tremendously. Yet, Ruth acknowledged one day that she had not really taken the time to think about herself in a sustained fashion; namely, how she felt about her own death. Soon afterward, Ruth joined a support group for women with breast cancer, a gathering of women that seemed to uplift her and give her the camaraderie that neither family or friends could provide. While she continued to see me on a regular basis, I realized that Ruth was coming to terms with her illness in a healthy manner and was seeking the various types of support that would help her deal with her own death. Each woman in the cancer support group that Ruth attended was expected to contribute in some way to the weekly discussions, a requirement that turned out to be a catalyst for her. Ruth began keeping a journal of poetry and prose to document the emotions she was feeling, a record of her illness that she shared with me and with her cancer support group. Furthermore, family and friends read the pieces she had created. By using her talents to give back to the community and share her experiences, Ruth was able to regain the self-esteem that had been eroded by her debilitating illness. The courage Ruth demonstrated working on this journal, a document that was eventually published and gained acclaim for its honest, reveals the positive potential that lies within the process of death and dying. Ruth's willingness to explore subjects that are often ignored or silenced reflected her desire to find hope, even in the face of death. Moreover, the functional family, one that invites discussion and debate, nurtures love, trust and respect among its members, remains an important place for such contributions to begin.

Mortality, both our own and that of our loved ones, poses a series of hurdles that must by faced and crossed throughout our lives. Though individual circumstances make the subject of death and dying a unique experience, we all share many of the same emotions, concerns, and thoughts about our own positions in life and the void left by those who have died. The death of a loved one reminds us of our own mortality in an immediate and often painful fashion. Yet, death and dying also provides survivors with the opportunity to reassess themselves and to gain understanding through loss. Although death always has a tragic and immediate impact on the family, it marks a chance to find hope in our own vitality and to learn from the memories of those who have died or are dying. The process of death and dying requires that we not only consider the way it was, but also examine the way it is, to bring new insight to one of the most fundamental things we face in life: death. The greatest tragedy in life is for those individuals who have been so extensively damaged by a death that hopelessness is the only solution. The greatest gift that we are given in life is to live out our lives with integrity and hope. Many people have demonstrated their courage to find meaning in their lives after tragedy. Here's to life, l'chaim!

CONCLUSION

After the Goodbyes Have Been Said.

The pain of grief is a much a part of living as the ecstacy of love, because it is the cost of commitment and the price we pay for closeness. As human beings we need to mourn in response to loss. If for any reason we cannot, chances are there will be emotional or physical problems. It is essential to recognise that, above all else, healing takes time.

A great many people may be surprised and frightened by the things they experience after the death of a loved one. They often find themselves denying the truth at first and it may take several days to fully realize that the person is really gone. If there has been some warning about the death the denial will not be as intense. If, on the other hand, the death was sudden and unexpected, it may take a while to give up the denial. At night a wife may reach out to touch her spouse because she has forgotten he is gone. This momentary memory lapse is just the mind's way of saying "I can't cope with this much pain all at once."

Once it has been accepted that a loved one has died, there may be physical reactions which have never been experienced, such as tightness in the throat, tension in the body, a sense of heaviness or a feeling of weakness. These are all part of the body's response to severe stress. People have described their grief as waves of distress lasting twenty minutes to one hour. At those times they may find themselves crying or sighing; sometimes they feel tired, and at other times restless; they cannot eat and may even lose their sexual feelings. These feelings are perfectly normal after the death of someone close. Try to understand these feelings don't rush them away.

During the first few weeks of bereavement many people have a strong impulse to search for and find the dead person. Although they know it's pointless, they may still find themselves taking a second look in their child's favorite playground to make sure she isn't there; or following someone on the street who looks like their dead wife.

The survivors may find themselves preoccupied with thoughts of the dead person and the events leading up to and after death. They may not be able to erase from their mind the image of how the person looked when they died. It is a time when one is vulnerable and it seems difficult to go on.

The agony of losing a loved one and the accompanying anger all add up to make this the toughest period in our lives. It's made worse because we are forced to restructure our lives at a time when we are at our weakest. Sometimes the pain seems constant, especially in cases of suicide when many survivors suffer an enormous amount of guilt. Some people may even contemplate suicide themselves as a way to stop the hurting.

But regardless of the pain, we have a responsibility to live. The only way to get even with pain is to become a better and stronger person in the present. This doesn't mean we try to compete with the dead person, but take some of the good of the deceased to inspire us to the highest ideals. This period of intense pain is just temporary for most people, and in time the survivors will regain their strength and identity.

Some people adopt the traits, mannerisms or symptoms of the dead person during their bereavement. This behaviour can be explained. For some people it is so hard to say goodbye that copying the dead person's behaviour allows them to keep part of the deceased with them. This can also happen to children who have been close to a parent and cannot let go. The other explanation is that some people feel relieved the death has occurred but can't admit this to themselves or others. Because they feel guilty about their relief, they unwittingly begin to imitate the dead person's behaviour.

Many people are often surprised at the intensity of their feelings during the second week of bereavement. Most people find that the peak of grief occurs after the funeral is over and the family have all dispersed. This is the time to have a close friend or relative take over some of the household chores and responsibilities to leave time for the bereaved person to grieve.

The bereaved will appreciate any help a friend or relative can offer. Quietly assisting around the house in a non demanding way is a great help. So is encouraging the bereaved to show their anger and hurt in an uninhibited way.

People do not like to be pitied, but prefer simple expressions of sorrow. Telling them about your sorrow, about your understanding, of their turmoil and offering to help in any way, can be the most touching gift.

Although flowers are customary, it may be better to spend money in a donation to the cancer fund if the person died of cancer, or the heart fund if he or she died of heart disease. Those living nearby might like to bring the family a cake or some other food they have prepared. Such gestures are readily appreciated. Above all, however, let the bereaved know that they can call on you, because this is the time when they need to know that others are around to help.

The length of bereavement varies from person to person, but in general most people are ready to start a new life after about one year. However, as I have pointed out throughout the book, some people display prolonged or excessive grief. This can be a result of their own emotional problems or unresolved problems that existed in their relationship with the deceased. Some people grieve for years, until their friends and family are tired of sympathizing with them.

Friends and family may find it difficult when survivors extend their mourning and become demanding and dependant. Attempts to provide comfort may leave people feeling frustrated because they can't make the survivor feel better. Or, they may get so exasperated, they get angry with the grieving person. They may also feel guilty if they don't want to spend time with the person. Giving support can be very trying but just try to listen and think before you react. Regardless of how we feel, the survivor needs our comfort and respect.

Other survivors may not be able to grieve at all, or their grief might emerge in a distorted form. People having problems grieving should seek professional help. Grieving is an essential part of dealing with death and failing to grieve, or failing to stop grieving, may leave the survivors with serious psychological consequences.

Sooner or later we all have to cope with death. One day we will all die, our friends and relatives will die and new people will take our place. Coping with death may be life's most difficult task. For a married couple, it means the need of a very special relationship; for parents, losing a child means losing part of themselves and their stake in the future. If we spend our lives building trust, love and respect for another person, we cannot bear to see that person die because part of us dies too.

However, grief can bring strength and maturity to the survivors, showing us how very precious life is. It's something we can easily forget when everything is going well. Losing someone close makes us look at our own lives in a new light because suddenly we realize that we too could die at any time. It forces us to reassess where we are going in life and it might cause us to change in a very positive way. After a death, the reconciliation with life is important. After the goodbyes have been said we must be prepared to laugh and love again. No person can ever be replaced; he or she will always have a special place in the minds and hearts of friends and family. However, don't be afraid to meet new people or establish new relationships.

We all know death is inevitable and to have the courage to face our own death is to have the courage to face life. If at the end we can look back and say, "I did the best I could," we can face death peacefully. Coping with death is really coping with life.

REFERENCES

(Edited by) **Altschul, M.D.**, Sol, *Childhood Bereavement and Its Aftermath*, International University Press, Madison, Connecticut, 1989.

(Edited by) **Anthony, M.D., E. James and Koupernik, M.D., Cyrille**, *The Child in His Family: The Impact of Disease and Death*, John Wiley & Sons, New York, 1973.

Becker, Ernest, *The Denial of Death*, The Free Press, A Division of Macmillan Publishing Co. Inc., New York, 1978.

Bloom-Feshbach, Jonathan, Bloom-Feshbach, Sally, and Associates, *The Psychology of Separation and Loss*, Jossey Bass Publishers, San Francisco, 1987.

Boszormeny-Nagy, M.D., Ivan, Spark, M.S.W., Geraldine M., *Invisible Loyalties*, Harper and Row, Publishers, Inc., Hagerstown, Maryland, 1973.

Bright, R., *Grieving: A Handbook For Those Who Care*, Magna Music Batan Music Inc., St. Louis, MO, 1986

(Edited by) **Cain, Ph.D., Albert C.**, *Survivors of Suicide*, Charles C. Thomas, Springfield, Illinois, 1972.

Dietrich, D.R. & Shabad, P. (Eds.), *The Problem of Loss and Mourning: Psychoanalytic Perspectives*, International Universities Press, Madison, CT. 1990

Furman, Erna, *A Child's Parent Dies*, Yale University Press, New Haven and London, 1974.

(Edited by) **Grollman, Earl A.**, *Explaining Death to Children*, Beacon Press, Boston, 1967.

Group for the Advancement of Psychiatry, *Normal Adolescence: its Dynamics and Impact*, Charles Scribner's Sons, New York, 1968.

Krupnick, J.L., & Solomon, F., *Death of a Parent or Sibling During Childhood*, Jossey Bass, San Francisco 1987

Kubler-Ross, Elizabeth, *On Death and Dying*, MacMillan Publishing Co., Inc., New York, 1969.

Kubler-Ross, Elizabeth, *Death, The Final Stage of Growth*, Prentice Hall, Inc., New Jersey, 1975.

Kushner, Harold, *When Bad Things Happen to Good People*, Avon Books, New York, 1983.

Langone, John, *Death is a Noun*, Little, Brown and Company, Boston and Toronto, 1972.

Lidz, Theodore, *The Person, His Development Throughout the Life Cycle*, Basic Books Inc., New York, 1968.

Lifton, Robert Jay and Olson, Eric, *Living and Dying*, Praeger Publishers Inc., New York, 1974.

Parkes, Colin Murray, *Bereavement: Studies of Grief in Adult Life*, International Universities Press, New York, 1972.

Pincus, Lily, *Death and the Family*, Pantheon Books, A Division of Random House, New York, 1974.

Pollock, G., *The Mourning-Liberation Process*, International Universities Press, Vols. 1-2, Madison, CT, 1989.

(Edited by) **Ruitenbeck, Ph.D., Hendrik M.**, *The Interpretation of Death*, Jason Aronson Inc., New York, 1978.

Scarf, Maggie, *Intimate Partners*, Random House, New York, 1987.

(Edited by) **Schoenberg, Bernard, Carr, Arthur C., Kutscher, Austin H., Peretz, David, Goldberg, Ivan**, *Anticipatory Grief*, Columbia University Press, New York, 1974.

Weisman, M.D., Avery D., *On Dying and Denying*, Behavioral Publications Inc., New York, 1972.

Westley, William A., and Epstein Nathan B., *The Silent Majority*, Jossey Bass Inc., San Francisco, 1969.

Wylie, Betty Jane, *Beginnings: A Book for Widows*, McClelland and Stewart, Toronto, 1985.

(Edited by) **Zisook, S.**, *Biopsychosocial Aspects of Bereavement*, American Psychiatric Press, Washington, DC, 1987

Printed in the USA
CPSIA information can be obtained
at www.ICGtesting.com
JSHW082211140824
68134JS00014B/567